DECORATE YOUR HOME FOR *Christmas*

DECORATE YOUR HOME FOR
Christmas

JANA WILSON

Sterling Publishing Co., Inc. New York
A Sterling/Chapelle Book

FOR CHAPELLE LTD.

Owner
Jo Packham

Staff
Malissa Boatwright • Rebecca Christensen
Holly Fuller • Amber Hansen • Holly Hollingsworth
Susan Jorgensen • Susan Laws • Amanda McPeck
Barbara Milburn • Pat Pearson • Leslie Ridenour
Cindy Rooks • Cindy Stoeckl • Nancy Whitley

Photography
Kevin Dilley for Hazen Photography

Styling
Jo Packham

Chapelle Ltd. would like to thank Mary Gaskill of Trends n' Traditions, Connie Duran of The Loft on 25th., Jana Wilson of the VeeBar Guest Ranch and the Country Junction, LInda Durbano of the Snowy Range Cattle Company, and Ryne Hazen of Hazen Photography.

If you have any questions or comments or would like information on specialty products featured in this book, please contact:
Chapelle, Ltd., Inc., PO Box 9252, Ogden, UT 84409
801-621-2777 (phone), 801-621-2788 (fax).

Library of Congress Cataloging-in Publication Data

Wilson, Jana.
    Decorate your home for Christmas / Jana Wilson.
        p.   cm.
    "A Sterling/Chapelle book."
    Includes index.
    ISBN 0-8069-4295-9
    1. Christmas decorations. 2. Handicraft.   1. Title.
TT900.C4W55   1996
745.594'12--dc20   96-17720
                                                                                        CIP

1 3 5 7 9 10 8 6 4 2

A Sterling/Chapelle Book

First paperback edition published in 1997 by
Sterling Publishing Company, Inc.
387 Park Avenue South, New York, N.Y. 10016
© 1996 by Chapelle Limited
Distributed in Canada by Sterling Publishing
℅ Canadian Manda Group, One Atlantic Avenue, Suite 105
Toronto, Ontario, Canada M6K 3E7
Distributed in Great Britain and Europe by Chrysalis Books
64 Brewery Road, London N7 9NT, England
Distributed in Australia by Capricorn Link (Australia) Pty Ltd.
P.O. Box 704, Windsor, NSW 2756 Australia
Printed in China
All rights reserved

Sterling ISBN 0-8069-4295-9 Trade
1-4027-0098-9 Paper

Contents

JANA WILSON

As a mother, wife, designer, artist, and young entrepreneur, Jana feels that "Home is where the heart is." Helping others understand and enjoy this feeling in their own homes is why she shares her holiday season here.

JANA WILSON

Jana, her husband and three children, live on her family's working cattle ranch. &ᐧᗢ She also spends a great deal of time sharing many of her talents with her parents on their guest ranch. &ᐧᗢ Whether making something for herself or for her family, Jana's Christmas decorating and crafting ideas are often influenced by, and representative of, the people and the landscape that surround her.

When holiday guests arrive at the guest ranch they are welcomed by a large roaring fire and many of Jana's handmade decorations. Muslin Santas with mop beards are found on the mantle, sitting on antique spools. They fit perfectly behind Jana's Cowboy Kringle, Star & Tree Swag and underneath her natural grapevine wreath. When the holiday season is over, the wreath and spools remain. The Santas are replaced by other stuffed dolls that are indicative of the new season to be celebrated, and the wreath is decorated anew with dried flowers and ribbons.

INSTRUCTIONS FOR ITEMS FEATURED IN THIS SECTION ARE ON PAGES 71–75.

Holiday guests are delighted to see the attention to detail that is the trademark of Jana's decorating. Adjacent to the magazines on the coffee table, lay a pair of old ice skates. These much used, and much loved skates, bring forth images of happy and carefree days long past.

In her decorating, and for her craft projects, Jana likes to use those items that are most familiar to her—the objects that symbolize her life on the ranch. There is no better example of Jana's style than this seasonal wreath, in which she uses an old lariat, long since discarded by a ranch hand. She has added dried flowers from around the ranch and tied them together with a bow. Hanging inside the wreath is one of Jana's wooden Cowboy Boot Ornaments and next to the wreath hangs a knapsack. Jana changes the wreath with the seasons because with every season new flowers bloom around the ranch.

Jana, her family, and the ranch hands always cut their own Christmas tree from somewhere on their property. They keep the tree's original pine cones on the boughs. In this year's tree they found an abandoned bird's nest and left it to become a natural accent for her holiday decorations.

An easy accent to Jana's Cowboy Kringle Ornaments are Styrofoam balls wrapped with torn strips of bandanna fabric and then tied like miniature packages with jute bows.

Holiday table decorations are often a delightful surprise for family and friends. Above are a pair of tiny cowboy boots filled with holiday greenery. When living on a ranch, nothing is ever discarded—everything finds a new home and a new meaning.

When serving hot coffee to the guests at the ranch, a candy cane is always added for an unexpected flavor and a special touch of holiday cheer.

Behind Ropin' Cowboy Kringle Jana has hung an old, but still useful, knapsack. Guests are always fascinated with the "objects d'art" that Jana selects as perfect backdrops and accents for her seasonal decorations.

Decorations in unexpected places are always a delight to visitors. Here at the bottom of a wide stairway is an old trunk used to display holiday decor. Always staying with a theme, Jana wraps an empty package with fabric and ties it with traditional ribbons or strips of fabric.

Each detail must be attended to in the guest quarters. Here Jana has made tissue holders which compliment each room. They are so simple that Jana often sells them to the guests. She begins by selecting holiday or year-round fabric and simply cuts a 10" x 20" fabric rectangle; folds it in half and sews up two sides. She then follows the side seam down to the fold line on the bottom to make a triangle. She measures $2\frac{1}{4}$" from the tip of the triangle and marks a line across from side to side. She sews on the marked line on both sides to form the square corners for the box shape. She folds the top edge down $\frac{1}{2}$" and sews all around. She then makes a small slit—big enough to string jute or ribbon through. She cuts an 18"-length of jute and strings it through, gathering the fabric after the tissue box is inserted and tying it shut.

Jana also makes accent pillows for each season by wrapping old pillows in squares of fabric and knotting the ends.

JANA WILSON 13

debbie hardy

Featured here is the master suite of nationally renowned artist and designer, Debbie Hardy. Debbie's love of nature is evident in her works and in her surroundings.

debbie hardy

Having spent most of her youth around the fresh waters of streams and lakes, Debbie Hardy has always been able to connect with the wonderful colors of nature, both in and out of the water. ❧ Early in her life, Debbie found she was a natural at using a brush and a piece of paper to create beautiful images. ❧ She has pursued, expanded, and refined this talent throughout her adult life.

At the moment, Debbie is selling original art, prints, and t-shirts, and is active in sharing her talents with audiences and other artists. Past projects have included the watercolor Father Christmas seen here, but her current projects are completing her series of freshwater fish and introducing her collection of wildflowers.

INSTRUCTIONS FOR ITEMS FEATURED IN THIS SECTION ARE ON PAGES 76–81.

Adjacent to the master bedroom in Debbie's home is a jacuzzi with a fireplace—a perfect hideaway for her to relax, pamper herself, and find the time for the inspirations that are required to create her newest watercolors. Every detail of her bath area contributes to a surrounding that offers tranquility and artistic inspiration—even the large green-and-white-checkered towels are edged with matching trim.

So that every prized possession looks as though its colors are taken from the lakes and streams that she so dearly loves, Debbie paints everything with a watercolor wash. Purchased reed Santas, the baskets that hold her bath-time necessities and frivolities, and even the pine cones, placed inside the baskets, have been touched with the colors of the river. She surrounds the jacuzzi completely with trees and blushed pink poinsettias for the season, and allows only candle- and firelight to illuminate her private chamber.

LINDA CASSITY DURBANO

Linda draws most of her ideas from her surroundings. "It is great to have such a wonderful backdrop to decorate around. This home, with all its rustic beauty, inspires me to design decorations that compliment its rugged style."

LINDA CASSITY DURBANO

Linda lives with her husband, David, in a home that is a statement of their eclectic and active lifestyle. ✑ *Every room throughout their house displays treasures that were purchased while traveling; "antiques" that were rescued and renovated; objects created by artisans, some who are friends, others who are simply admired; and pieces that were stumbled upon in unpredictable places.*

One of Linda's talents is to convert any idea, no matter how obscure, into an actual project that is admired by all who see it. ✑ *She can change a dilapidated desk into a functional work of art, and can create tiny Christmas tree ornaments from twigs she finds in her yard.* ✑ *She rewrites the rules of art and decorating, carefully and innovatively creating an atmosphere for family and friends that is comfortable, fashionable, and always unanticipated!*

INSTRUCTIONS FOR ITEMS FEATURED IN THIS SECTION ARE ON PAGES 82–85.

MANY OF THE ANTIQUES in this home were abandoned by the previous owners. Each was salvaged and carefully restored to its original grandeur. One of the tables in the living room is actually a door with oxen yolk legs that dates back before the turn of the century.

LINDA BELIEVES THAT some projects should be lovingly and painstakingly completed so that they become family heirlooms. Others, however, like these Stand-Up Santas, should be made quickly, easily, and inexpensively so that multiples can be created and given to visiting friends.

"BACK TO NATURE" HAS ALWAYS been a priority for the Durbano's while at home in the foothills of the mountains. All of the doors at the ranch are handmade from beetle-kill pine harvested from a mountain peak near their home. Some, like the Tree Doors here, are accented with cutouts to bring indoors the wilderness they love so much.

BECAUSE LINDA AND DAVID SPEND most of their days out-of-doors many of her decorations, whether year round or especially for Christmas, are made from natural fibers and nature's gifts found along the river, in the meadows, or tucked away inside old structures on their property.

CONNIE DURAN

Like many young new shop owners, Connie spends almost as much time in her store as she does at home. For this reason, as well as for her customers, she exhibits little or no restraint when decorating for the holiday season. She understands that if the decorations look absolutely lovely in the store, they will be even more beautiful when taken home.

Connie Duran

Connie is a wife, homemaker, and mother of four children, who are mostly grown now. ❧ Connie worked in retail for many years, yet dreamed of one day having a shop of her own, one that would express her talents and her love for fun and uniqueness.

In a twist of fate, Connie happened upon a space tucked away at the top of the stairs of a historic building undergoing restoration. ❧ She knew instantly that this out-of-the-way space had somehow been waiting over a century for just the right person to bring it to life. ❧ Whether decorating for Christmas in her home or in her shop, Connie spends the majority of her time attending to the small details that make the holidays so special. ❧ For example, she believes that when serving holiday beverages to guests, they should be "presented" on a serving tray adorned with holiday finery.

*I*n one of the two rooms in her shop, Connie selected a theme of glass, gold, and candles for this year's celebrations. She believes that there is nothing more festive than the glow of candlelight during the holidays.

INSTRUCTIONS FOR ITEMS FEATURED IN THIS SECTION ARE ON PAGES 86–89.

*S*ome of us like the feel of country decorating; some prefer the roughness of primitive pieces; and some, like Connie, love the extravagance of elegance. And what could be more elegant than a master bedroom all dressed up for the holidays in cream and shades of gold? Here, on a bed most women dream of owning, are hand-made pillows and elegant throws that are watched over by hand cast Christmas angels.

ryne & teresa hazen

With Ryne's talent as a photographer and Teresa's talent for making everyone "picture perfect," the Hazen's home is decorated with photographs of family and friends. They feel that the accents in their home, whether on a wall or on their Christmas tree, should tell a story. Their decorations can be saved, used, and treasured for generations.

ryne & teresa hazen

Ryne, Teresa, and their two children, Tyrone and Toya, live in a house in which they display a unique style all their own. ✄ *They are collectors of memorabilia, but only items that can be used to provide an atmosphere conducive to a home filled with family and friends.* ✄ *The cola and 50s theme used in the dining room is an example of how memorabilia can help create a special place for both young and old.*

WHEN GUESTS WALK INTO THE Hazen dining room they are automatically transported to another time—one boasting bobby socks, felt skirts, and rockin' 'round the Christmas tree! Here, for friends and family, they have recreated a time for music, fun, and holiday celebrating.

INSTRUCTIONS FOR ITEMS FEATURED IN THIS SECTION ARE ON PAGES 90–93.

THE FOLLOWING ARE SOME ideas in which you can dress the purchased bears on the opposite page. Mrs. Clause is dressed in a red velvet hat and quaint little apron. Santa is also sporting a red velvet hat, trimmed with fur. Santa's helper is wearing a jester collar and hat to compliment his elf-like pointed ears. The reindeer bear has twig antlers, a red pom-pom nose, and a bell harness. "Tangled-up bear" is holding a miniature ladder and is wrapped with miniature lights. The snowman bear has a carrot nose, cape, buttons, and broom; and to top it all off, he is wearing a top hat! The angel bear is decorated with wings and a halo. The sleepy-time bear is wearing holiday pajamas with a matching cap.

TERESA TAKES GREAT DELIGHT IN decorating her bath area. With each new season she chooses new colors for her make-up, different types of skin care products, and different fragrances—all of which are very important to her; and with each of these changes comes a change in her bath area. For the holiday season the colors this year are bright, bold, and festive. The skin care products used to decorate the Bath Wreath are the same ones Teresa uses everyday. Teresa believes making a wreath for a friend is more festive than simply wrapping the products separately and delivering them in a traditional gift box.

TERESA'S BATH AREA IS QUITE SMALL so she stores and displays her everyday toiletries in a gift type basket—something her holiday guests always admire.

TERESA WOULD LIKE TO HAVE A huge bath area with not only room to store her necessities but with wall space to display her much loved art frivolities. Her bath area, however, is smaller than desired but her creativity and ingenuity use even this obstacle to the best advantage. Instead of displaying art painted on canvas and hung on the wall, she displays art created on cotton shower curtains. The curtains change with the season or a whim!

Penelope Hammons

Penelope is the mother of eight children, seven sons and one daughter. 🌿 *The Hammons' home has always been open to their children's friends.* 🌿 *Over 30 kids have lived with them from time to time, some for a week and others for over a year.*

Because of the constant arrival of a new family member or friend, decorating has been an avocation which has provided an opportunity for Penelope to share her talents with others. 🌿 *"Christmas has presented special decorating challenges, and through trial-and-error, some wonderful accomplishments."*

INSTRUCTIONS FOR ITEMS FEATURED
IN THIS SECTION ARE ON PAGES 94–96.

Penelope's home sits majestically perched high in the mountains and is surrounded not only by natural growth but also by well-tended gardens. Her love of nature and the gifts it so freely gives are what inspire a good portion of her home decorating—whether it be for a close friend's wedding or for Christmas. If guests look closely at the decorations on the tree in her downstairs family room, they will find the silver dollars that grow outside the front door and the baby's breath that are found on the hills outside the front window.

Penelope often gives demonstrations to people decorating on a shoe string. She recommends shopping for decorations after Christmas for great buys and using things from the yard for accents. For example, spray holly bush branches with gold paint or collect pine cones from the park and use them in place of purchased picks. "I always encourage individuals to put aside $15 to $20 a month throughout the year and use it to purchase one 'great' decorating item. In 10 years, you will have many quality pieces to enhance your home."

Displaying decorated gift bags is a simple idea that can add Christmas cheer to any room. Place a weight, such as a brick or rock, in the bottom of a decorative bag. Fill the bag with real or artificial pine branches. Add other odds and ends left over from decorating. Fill many bags and place them on shelves or stagger on steps as shown on page 43.

"I love sharing my talents with others. Each year at Christmastime, we open our home to visitors. People ask me, 'how can you let strangers peek through every nook and cranny of your home?' But if someone can be inspired by the things I do and make—that's wonderful!"

The poinsettias that decorate the tree in Penelope's master bedroom are one of her after-Christmas sale purchases. Because some of the flowers were a little worn they were simply sprayed with a generous coat of gold glitter. The lights from the tree make them sparkle like new!

There are several staircases in Penelope's house and the once empty spaces under each are her visitor's favorites. Each area under the stairs has been transformed into a magical world of miniatures. This little kitchen area is discovered by opening a miniature door, complete with stained glass window. Inside is a table set for dining, a miniature cast iron stove, and all of the accessories that any small guest might require. Penelope takes great pride in her miniature hideaways and decorates them from top to bottom for each and every holiday and season.

Every treasure that Penelope finds becomes a home for some decoration. This weathered child's wheelbarrow is the perfect place for poinsettias. In the spring she "plants" it with tulips and fall finds it overflowing with pumpkins and autumn leaves.

These pictures were purchased at an antique shop, but any Christmas print or art would work. Just stretch desired fabric over cardboard cut to fit inside a large frame. Staple or tape to back. Mount smaller frames inside. Hang a pine and berry spray over picture for a complete ensemble.

Another one of Penelope's "finds" is made extra special by the cute little hat that was quickly created, giving this little Santa an added air of whimsy.

Diane Watson

As a decorator and crafter Diane has developed her own unique style. Here, in Diane's formal dining room, her talent of attending to each detail is showcased.

Diane Watson

Diane and her husband, Gene, live in a home that was built in 1879. Today about 30 acres, a renovated log bunkhouse, an old barn, other outbuildings, and two trout ponds are all that remain.

"I guess we just like old things," Diane comments. "As you can see, nearly everything in this house was 'formerly owned' and found in flea markets or junk shops. Friends seem to relax more immediately when their surroundings are 'lived in' and we just don't worry about kids, dogs, mud, snow, or other distractions.

"Decorating for Christmas is great fun and really starts in the summer and fall when we scour nearby fields for interesting native materials to be stored for November and December. I supplement with a few dried flowers, greens, and ribbons purchased in town, but, otherwise I try to use what grows here. Actually, it's fun to see how differently you look at a meadow or a mountain when you're looking for something pretty to use indoors."

Diane is a designer who loves the secrecy of, and pays a great deal of attention to, every nook and cranny in her home. One of her favorite hideaways is the loft tucked above her dining room. Most of the walls in Diane's loft, as well as those in her living room, are covered from floor to ceiling with bookcases—all of which are crowded with publications on any subject imaginable. Because her loft is such a special place to her, Diane decorated the banister that quards it with one of her friend's favorite pieces —this much used and loved antique tuba! For Christmas entertaining, the tuba and banister are strung with garlands and beads so that guests who happen to look up see hints of holiday cheer.

Diane's dining room is at one end of what, in some places, is occasionally called "the great room" or "the lodge." She has tried to give the area a visual feeling of warmth and intimacy of space. Areas can be defined with the placement of the table and chairs, an area rug, collectables, or a color scheme. Diane has used a salmon color for one of her walls because it has a warm feel and compliments the patterns and colors in the paintings and oriental carpet. Another reason for her color choice is that she lives in a predominantly cool climate, so the visual "heat" is welcome. However, if one lives in a warm climate, a similar technique with a cooler color might be used.

This chandelier is a free-form project that depends on the light fixture available. Use three or four elements that will blend with the table setting and centerpiece. Some possibilities include use of bells, pine cones, pine boughs, fruit, ornaments, pieces of fabric, or ribbons.

INSTRUCTIONS FOR ITEMS FEATURED IN THIS SECTION ARE ON PAGES 97–98.

In decorating, the simplest objects can make a significant statement when done in multiples. Every decorator and crafter knows that it is just as easy to make several of something as it is to make one. In place of a single potted tree, Diane displays Three Dried Trees—simple but noteworthy.

Diane loves to decorate with small "surprising" touches, so much so that when guests arrive they have learned to expect the unexpected. A perfect example of this is the stacking of chairs in her living area. Most traditionalists use chairs for sitting—Diane uses hers for accentuating! Here she uses them to showcase a gift for the guest of honor as it rests atop a miniature chair.

The coffee table in Diane's living room is an indoor display of the natural materials which grow in the foothills around her house. In this Bark Tree and Basket Centerpiece, antique carrier bark, berries, and dried willow buds become as elegant as their indoor surroundings with the addition of a garland of tiny, white pearls.

The wood-burning stove in Diane's living room is always ablaze in the winter. Candles that decorate the mantle and table tops are lit for special occasions. Diane and her husband like the the cozy feeling of being inside while they sit and read or share a quiet moment together, but it is more important to them that everyone who enters feels equally as warm, as welcome, and "at home."

Diane may live in a rugged countryside, but she loves all things elegant and delicate. It is difficult to surround herself on a day-to-day basis with such finery, so decorating her tree for the holidays with fragile treasures is a special treat. Her tree sparkles with small lights and is exquisitely adorned with tiny rosebuds and lace. It is a touch of gentleness in a land that is wild and harsh.

Mary Gaskill

"In 1984 my father and I pooled our resources and talents to fill a void after the loss of my mother. *We started a little woodworking business which later developed into the present establishment that sells gifts and collectables.

The gift shop no longer carries any of our earlier woodwork, but has opened up to a wide variety of interests, and features the work of artisans and craftspeople from everywhere."

Every square inch of Mary's shop in a renovated building is filled with floral arrangements, collectables, furniture, baskets, gourmet food, jewelry, and more. *Every season offers new experiences and delights but Christmas is everyone's favorite . *There are trees decorated throughout the store each adorned with tiny works of art.

A store the size of Mary's is a commitment in time, energy, and emotion. *"I have never regretted the investment" says Mary,"I have grown immensely from the association with those who have cared about, believed in, and supported all of my endeavors.

INSTRUCTIONS FOR ITEMS FEATURED IN THIS SECTION ARE ON PAGE 99.

Lindsey Hale

Lindsey is one of the artists who supplies designs to Mary's shop. ❧ She loves her work, but even more, loves the fact that she can balance it with her family life as a wife and mother of four children.

Being born into an artistic family sparked her interest in designing, which for the past eight years has been directed in the area of floral design.

Specializing in wreaths, garlands, and table arrangements, Lindsey uses many different mediums such as silk, latex, dried, and preserved flowers. ❧ "As a designer, I love Christmas—there is a never-ending supply of banisters, mantles, and doors that need that holiday touch."

Nadine Farley

Nadine feels that she came into this life blessed with a great deal of creativity, a God-given gift that she considers to be her greatest asset.

As a child she was always playing make believe, living in a world of her own. ✆ *Today, her ability to use her imagination and creativity to produce things of joy for others is evident in her beautiful ornaments.* ✆ *"My work helps me to express my emotions —how I feel about life."*

Nadine is also one of the artists that exhibits and sells her wares at Mary's shop. Her uncommon approach to floral and fruit baskets is one that is much sought after.

Different varieties of Nadine's decorated ornaments are shown here. Notice how simple details add to the elegance of each piece.

rap a colorful ball ornament with gold netting. Decorate top as desired with items such as assorted trims, fabrics, berries, dried flowers, greenery, and pine cones. Hang each with matching ribbon.

o make these beautiful and fragrant ornaments, glue potpourri to a ball ornament and hang with gold cording. These ornaments may be waxed as those on the previous page.

Jo Packham

Jo is the mother of two and president of Chapelle Ltd., a company that authors and packages how-to books on every craft imaginable. ❧ Another important branch of the company is The Vanessa-Ann Collection, which draws from the talents of many in-house and free-lance designers to produce new designs, techniques, and concepts for crafters. ❧ Because books must be finished in the spring to be ready for release in the fall, it is Christmastime nearly year round at Vanessa-Ann's offices.

In this chapter, Jo and her designers decorate several homes, each with a unique style and theme. ❧ Jo's own home always has four or five different trees and distinctive decorations in every nook and cranny.

The Christmas themes in Jo's home vary from year to year and are oftentimes inspired by the most unexpected sources. ❧ In years past, branches of trees have been laden with miniature sporting-goods equipment, handmade Victorian jesters, elegant fabric-covered teapots, and hand-painted glass ornaments.

INSTRUCTIONS FOR ITEMS FEATURED IN THIS SECTION ARE ON PAGES 100–125.

"I LOVE THE HOLIDAYS" says Jo, "and so I do whatever I can to make the season special and memorable for myself, my family, and our friends."

Every Christmas brings new ideas for celebrating and decorating. Rather than a traditional Christmas each year in the little Tudor home nestled at the base of the mountains, the tradition has become to do something different with each passing year.

This year the trees in the living room are decorated especially for Jo's daughter Sara. Even though she is a sophomore in college, Sara loves the fairy tales that were read to her as a child—Cinderella is one of her favorites.

ONE OF THE CHRISTMAS trees is left natural and decorated with the wicked stepsisters and the lovable objects that surrounded Cinderella while she lived with her wicked stepmother. When friends bring their children by to see the trees, they see the brooms Cinderella swept with, the mice and tiny birds that kept her company, the moon and stars she wished upon, and the pumpkins that were to become so important. Everyone's favorite, however, are the wicked stepsisters and their mother. These wonderful cloth dolls were designed and created by internationally acclaimed artisan Julie McCullough. The base of the tree is surrounded by gift packages wrapped with brown craft paper and tied with string. There are also baskets of pumpkins, apples, and oranges; Stick Bundles; and stuffed teddy bears that are Cinderella's secret friends.

THE SECOND PINE tree is blanketed in a layer of snow and stardust glitter and decorated for Cinderella at the ball. The ornaments are Cinderella's Slipper Ornaments, the lights are wedding bells with tiny birds attached, and there are Cinderella's Coach Ornaments on the branches. The tree is strung with glass beads and crystal ornaments and is watched over by Cinderella's Fairy Godmother Tree Top.

The packages under the tree are placed on a layered lace tree skirt that could have been Cinderella's petticoat and are wrapped in the invitations to the ball.

You are cordially
invited to attend a

Royal Ball

by Order of the Prince

Time:

8 o'clock p.m.

Place:

The Royal Palace
of HRH the Prince

RSVP

WHEN JO decorates for Christmas no detail is too important and too much is never enough! For that reason the decorations on and under the tree are attended to with great care and deliberation. Each Slipper Ornament has to be different and the cushions that hold them are made from small pieces of velvet that Jo has collected over the years. Cinderella's Tree Skirt is created from pieces of lace collected from around the country or found in an old trunk.

THE MANTLE THAT greets family and guests is decorated with treasured crystal candlesticks. Jo's oldest, closest friend gives her one new candlestick every year for Christmas, so they are always the center of her Christmas decorating. The Floral and Cuffed Stockings are made with ribbons and antique velvet flowers. However, the Coach Planters that hold her favorite pink poinsettias are, she felt, her most creative contribution! They are made from plastic Halloween pumpkins that children carry their candy in!

Jo is President of Chapelle Ltd. and The Vanessa-Ann Collection but she emphasizes over and over again that she is only one member of a most incredible and creative team. She, herself, loves old and much loved treasures and her home is the very definition of "eclectic." However, the other designers at Chapelle each have their own personalized design ideas. When Susan Laws and Cindy Rooks were asked to create a "Christmas Wonderland" for the office's controller, Holly Hollingsworth, they turned to country. Holly and her husband, James', new home is 46 years old and was recently renovated by the two of them and an undetermined number of family members. For Holly and James' first Christmas in their new home, Susan and Cindy filled their living room with the magic of a simple, country Christmas.

The Revolving Reindeer that sits in the middle of their mantle is actually a music box that entertains Holly's nephew for hours. The Snowman and Santa Stocking Holders are each attached to purchased metal stocking holders and each hold a garland of seasonal gifts and goodies.

THE LITTLE LOG HOUSE that sits by the fireplace is filled with tiny treasures and treats for friends and family. This piece is Holly's favorite and will definitely find a place in her new home for each holiday throughout the year.

THESE LARGE stockings are so popular they were made in two sizes. Medium-sized stockings can be used for decorating the entire month of December. Large-sized stockings can be hung on Christmas eve, so Santa will have plenty of room to leave all of his gifts!

ONE OF SUSAN'S favorite techniques is to combine fabric and paint. Even though this particular Santa has painted plaid cuffs, Susan is certain they would be even cuter if the plaid was fabric and decoupaged on.

A THIRD THEME created by the Vanessa-Ann team is one for a warm and wooly Christmas. Chapelle's Vice President, Becky Christensen, and her family love the out-of-doors and are very active in a variety of sports. These decorations are a perfect compliment to their active life-styles. On the tree in the family room are hand-knitted sweaters that are miniature replicas once owned by Becky's children. The window is painted with the snowman they build together every year as a family.

BUCKAROO SNOWMAN

MATERIALS

Bandanna: red
Raffia
Acrylic paints: black, gold, maroon, metallic silver, rust, and antique white
Acrylic matte spray sealer
Wiping stain: maple
Permanent marker, fine-point: black
Pine board: $3/4$" x 16" x 16" (1), $1/4$" x 5" x 5" (1)
Twigs: 2
Wire: 22 gauge (46")

GENERAL SUPPLIES

Cotton swab
Craft knife
Drill with $1/8$" drill bit
Jigsaw
Paintbrushes: thin and medium
Pliers
Sandpaper
Wire cutters
Wood glue

INSTRUCTIONS

1. Enlarge patterns (right) 400%. From $3/4$" pine, cut out snowman and two boots. From $1/4$" pine, cut out star and carrot nose.

2. Drill holes marked on patterns. Using craft knife, carve detail lines in hat. Sand all wood and wipe clean. Stain back sides of all wood.

3. Paint snowman referring to patterns. To paint cheeks, dip cotton swab in maroon paint and

blot until almost dry. Brush swab on cheek area to be blushed; let dry.

4. Glue carrot nose in place with wood glue. Draw details on carrot with black marker. When dry, spray painted wood with acrylic sealer.

5. Attach boots to snowman with 6" of wire in each hole. Twist ends with pliers to secure. Cut a 28" length of wire for hanger. Curve wire and thread ends into holes on each side of hat. Twist ends. Hang star from hanger with a 6" length of wire.

6. Glue twig to each side forming arms. Cut bandanna in half diagonally. Tie bandanna around neck, rolling straight edge under several times to shorten. Tie a raffia bow at top of hanger. ❧

**ENLARGE
PATTERNS 400%**

LARIAT WREATH
(Photo on opposite page)

MATERIALS

Old rope
Baby's breath sprigs
Eucalyptus sprigs
Fabric ribbon: green, red (4 yds. each)
Fine wire

INSTRUCTIONS

1. Coil rope to desired size of wreath. Secure coil with wire at sides and bottom.

2. Place eight to nine sprigs of eucalyptus at each side of wreath. Make a bow with both colors of ribbon. Secure sprigs and bow with wire at bottom of wreath. Add baby's breath throughout wreath. ❧

Drill Hole

Drill Hole

Drill Hole

Drill Holes

COWBOY BOOT ORNAMENT

MATERIALS

Raffia
Acrylic paints: black, dk. green, maroon, and metallic silver
Acrylic matte spray sealer
Wiping stain: maple
Pine board: $3/4$" x 10" x 7"
Wire: 22 gauge (18")

GENERAL SUPPLIES

Drill with $1/8$" drill bit
Jigsaw
Paintbrushes: fine and medium
Sandpaper
Wire cutters

INSTRUCTIONS

1. Enlarge boot pattern (page 71) 400%. From $3/4$" pine, cut one boot. Drill holes in top of boot as marked on pattern. Sand wood and stain back side.

2. Paint boot referring to pattern or as desired; let dry. Spray with acrylic sealer.

3. Thread wire through hole in top of boot. Bend ends. Tie raffia bow at top of hanger. Hang alone or inside of rope wreath. ❧

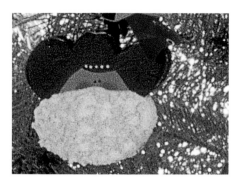

COWBOY KRINGLE ORNAMENT

MATERIALS

Bandanna: red
Raffia
Acrylic paints: beige, black, gold, maroon, metallic silver, and antique white
Acrylic matte spray sealer
Wiping stain: maple
Pine board: $3/4$" x 6" x 6" and $1/4$" x 3" x 3" (for each ornament)
Wire: 22 gauge (12" each ornament)

GENERAL SUPPLIES

Cotton swab
Craft knife
Drill with $1/8$" drill bit
Jigsaw
Paintbrushes: fine, medium, and stencil
Pliers
Sandpaper
Wire cutters

INSTRUCTIONS

1. Enlarge patterns (right) 200%. From $3/4$" pine, cut out desired number of Santas. From $1/4$" pine, cut out same number of stars.

2. Drill holes as marked on patterns. Carve hat details with craft knife. Sand pieces and stain backs.

3. Paint pieces referring to patterns. To paint cheeks, dip cotton swab in maroon paint and blot until almost dry. Brush swab on cheek area to be blushed. To achieve fluffy texture for beard, mix some fine sawdust, antique white paint, and water to oatmeal consistency. (Note: A purchased snow texturizing medium can be substituted here.) Dab onto beard trim with a stencil brush; let dry for several hours. Sand edges as desired. Spray with acrylic sealer.

4. Cut one 8" and one 4" length of wire for each ornament. Curve 8" wire and thread ends through drill holes in hat. Twist ends with pliers to secure. Thread one end of 4" wire into drill hole in star. Twist end to secure. Twist other end onto center of hanger.

5. Tie a strip of bandanna fabric and a few raffia strands around each hanger. ❧

ENLARGE PATTERNS 200%

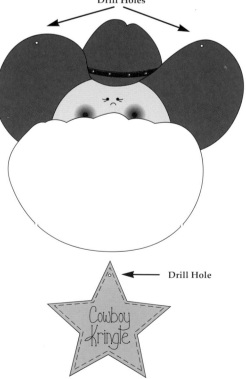

Drill Holes

Drill Hole

Cowboy Kringle

ROPIN' COWBOY KRINGLE

MATERIALS

Bandanna: red
Raffia
Twine: 36"
Acrylic paints: beige, black, blue, gold, indigo, maroon, metallic silver, and antique white
Acrylic matte spray sealer
Wiping stain: maple
Pine board: ³/₄" x 9" x 12" (1), ¹/₄" x 3" x 3" (1)
Wire: 22 gauge (60")

GENERAL SUPPLIES

Cotton swab
Craft knife
Drill with ¹/₈" drill bit
Jigsaw
Paintbrushes: fine, medium, and stencil
Pliers
Sandpaper
Wire cutters

INSTRUCTIONS

1.   Enlarge patterns (right) 300%. From ³/₄" pine, cut out body and legs. From ¹/₄" pine, cut out star.

2.   Drill holes as marked on pattern. Carve detail into hat with craft knife. Sand pieces and stain backs.

3.   Paint pieces referring to patterns. To paint cheeks, dip cotton swab in maroon paint and blot until almost dry. Brush swab on cheek area to be blushed. To achieve fluffy texture for beard and trim, mix some fine sawdust, antique white paint, and water to oatmeal consistency. (Note: A purchased snow texturizing medium can be substituted here.) Dab onto beard and trim with a stencil brush; let dry for several hours. Sand edges as desired. Spray with acrylic sealer.

4.   Wrap a three-looped coil in one end of twine. Attach coil through hole in lower hand with a 4" length of wire. Bring the remaining twine up across chest into upper hand. Twist an 18" length of wire into a lasso shape and secure ends into upper hand hole. Weave twine around wire lasso and secure at base with a knot.

5.   Attach legs with a 6" length of wire. Thread an 18" length of wire through holes in hat and twist ends, forming hanger. Attach star to top of hanger with a 4" length of wire.

6.   Tie raffia and bandanna to top of hanger. ❧

Drill Hole

ENLARGE PATTERNS 300%

Drill Holes

Drill Holes

Drill Holes

COWBOY SANTA STAR

Materials

Raffia
Acrylic paints: beige, black, dk.
    green, maroon, metallic silver,
    and antique white
Acrylic matte spray sealer
Wiping stain: maple
Pine board: $^3/_4$" x 8" x 6" (1),
    1 $^1/_4$" x 4 $^1/_2$" x 3 $^1/_2$" (1 for base)
Wooden dowel: $^1/_4$" x 5"

General supplies

Cotton swab
Craft knife
Drill with $^1/_4$" drill bit
Jigsaw
Paintbrushes: fine, medium, and
    stencil
Sandpaper
Wood glue

Instructions

1.   Enlarge one of the patterns (right) 200%. From $^3/_4$" pine, cut out one Santa.

2.   Drill a $^1/_4$" hole between legs of Santa. Drill a $^1/_4$" hole in center of base. Carve hat details with craft knife. Sand pieces and stain base and dowel.

3.   Paint front and back pieces referring to patterns. To paint cheeks, dip cotton swab in maroon paint and blot until almost dry. Brush swab on cheek area to be blushed. To achieve fluffy texture for beard and trim, mix some fine sawdust, antique white paint, and water to oatmeal consistency. (Note: A purchased snow texturizing medium can be substituted here.) Dab onto beard and trim with a stencil brush; let dry for several hours. Sand edges as desired.

4.   Place a drop of wood glue on both ends of dowel. Insert dowel in base and in Santa. Spray all wood with acrylic sealer.

5.   Tie a few strands of raffia around dowel. ❧

**ENLARGE
ONE OF THE
PATTERNS 200%**

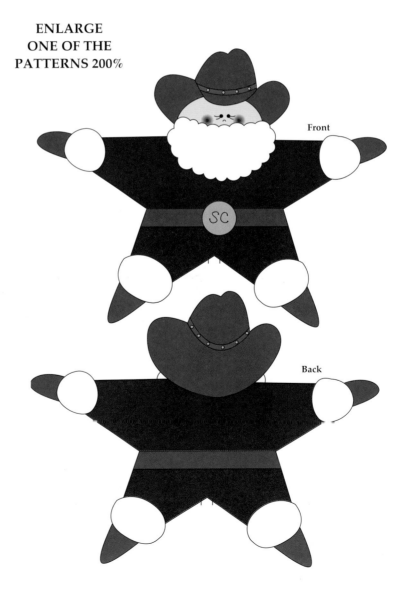

COWBOY KRINGLE, STAR & TREE SWAG

Materials

Bandanna: red
Raffia
Acrylic paints: beige, black, brown,
    dk. green, gold, maroon,
    metallic silver, and antique
    white
Acrylic matte spray sealer
Wiping stain: maple
Pine board: $3/4$" x 6" x 18" (1),
    $1/4$" x 4" x 12" (1)
Wire: 22 gauge (62")

General Supplies

Cotton swab
Craft knife
Drill with $1/16$" drill bit
Jigsaw
Paintbrushes: thin, medium, and
    stencil
Pliers
Sandpaper
Wire cutters

Instructions

1.   Enlarge patterns (right) 200%.
From $3/4$" pine, cut three Santas.

From $1/4$" pine, cut two stars and
two Christmas trees.

2.   Drill holes marked on
patterns. Using craft knife, carve

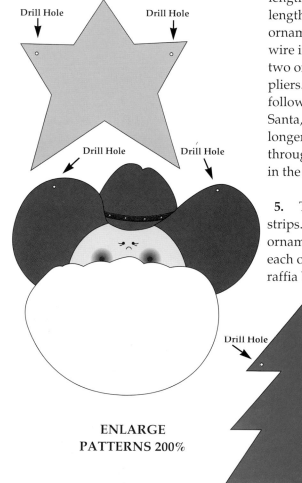

**ENLARGE
PATTERNS 200%**

detail in hat. Sand all wood and
wipe clean. Stain backs of projects.

3.   Paint pieces referring to
patterns. To paint cheeks, dip
cotton swab in maroon paint and
blot until almost dry. Brush swab
on cheek area to be blushed. To
achieve fluffy texture for beard, mix
some fine sawdust, antique white
paint, and water to oatmeal
consistency. (Note: A purchased
snow texturizing medium can be
substituted here.) Dab onto beard
with a stencil brush. Let dry for
several hours. Sand edges as
desired. Spray all wood with acrylic
sealer.

4.   Cut six 8" lengths and two 11"
lengths of wire. Use the shorter
lengths of wire to hold inside
ornaments together. Thread the
wire into the drill holes between
two ornaments and twist ends with
pliers. Assemble swag in the
following order: star, Santa, tree,
Santa, tree, Santa, star. Attach the
longer lengths of wire to each end
through holes in stars. Make a loop
in the end to use as a hanger.

5.   Tear bandanna into small
strips. Tie a strip between each
ornament. Tie some raffia between
each ornament. For the ends, tie a
raffia bow. 🍂

candle holder boxes

MATERIALS

(For one box)

Acrylic paints: black, blue, brown, burgundy, cream, gold, dk. green, tan, and white
Acrylic matte spray sealer
Pine board: 1/2" x 27" x 9"
Small finishing nails

GENERAL SUPPLIES

Hammer
Paintbrushes: fine, medium, and large
Sandpaper
Scrollsaw
Sponge

INSTRUCTIONS

1. Enlarge desired box patterns (right) 400%. Trace desired pattern pieces onto pine. Cut out two side pieces, one front and back piece, and one 4 1/2" square for bottom piece. (Note: Side patterns are the narrow patterns without the fish design.)

2. Cut out scrollwork with scrollsaw. Sand all wood.

3. To assemble box, nail side pieces between front and back pieces. Drop bottom into box and nail in place.

4. Sponge-paint outside of box with dark green paint. Let dry. Paint inside of box cream.

5. Paint fish onto front of box. (Note: A fish cut-out may be decoupaged onto box following manufacturer's instructions on decoupage glue.) If this method is used, the entire box must be covered with the decoupage glue to provide an even finish.

6. Spray box with acrylic sealer. ❧

ENLARGE PATTERNS 400%

Style 1	Style 2	Style 3

stick frame ornament

MATERIALS

Small fish picture or color
    photocopy of the art below
Twine
Sticks (see note in Step 1)

GENERAL SUPPLIES

Craft knife
Hot glue gun and glue sticks

INSTRUCTIONS

1. Cut two sticks 8" long and two sticks 5 1/4" long. (Note: Length of sticks may vary depending on size of picture used.)

2. Cross sticks to form frame for picture. Mark each stick at the place that it needs to connect to the other.

3. Wrap twine around the intersections to hold frame together. Knot securely on back.

4. Tie a twine loop at top of frame to use as hanger. Hot-glue picture to back of frame. ❧

dried floral wreath

MATERIALS

Twig wreath
Assorted drieds: hydrangeas,
    leaves, and flowers
Pussy willows

GENERAL SUPPLIES

Hot glue gun and glue sticks

INSTRUCTIONS

Glue pussy willows randomly between wound twigs. Glue leaves and hydrangeas at bottom of wreath. Fill with other flowers by inserting in place without glue. ❧

fish & pole ornament

MATERIALS

Stick: 8" long
Sculpting clay
Raffia
Acrylic paint: desired colors
Acrylic matte spray sealer

GENERAL SUPPLIES

Hot glue gun and glue sticks
Paintbrushes: fine and medium
Oven

INSTRUCTIONS

1. Mold tiny fish from clay and bake following manufacturer's instructions. Paint fish as desired and seal with acrylic spray. (Note: Purchased fish charms may be used.)

2. Wrap a few strands of raffia around stick and hot-glue one or two fish onto raffia tails. ❧

ENLARGE ART 120%

fisherman's catch

MATERIALS

Fish fabric panels: 2 (model used
    13 $^3/_4$" x 8 $^1/_2$")
Muslin fabric: 12" x 10"
Fleece: 12" x 10"
Braid: rust, $^1/_8$" wide ($^3/_4$ yd.);
    rose/seafoam, $^3/_8$" wide (1 yd.)
Matching thread
Glass pebble beads
Iridescent bugle beads: $^1/_4$" long
    (small package)

GENERAL SUPPLIES

Beading needle
Scissors
Sewing machine

INSTRUCTIONS

1.   Cut fish shapes from fabric
panels. Using fish as a pattern, cut
two each from fleece and muslin.
Layer as follows: muslin fish (right
side up), rust braid (horizontally
across fish shape with 1"
overlapping mouth), fabric panel
fish (right side down), fleece fish.
Starting at one side of tail, sew all
layers together, finishing at other
side of tail and leaving bottom of
tail open. Pull braid gently to turn
fish right side out. Repeat for
second fish using other end of
braid. (Note: Braid should be kept
in one piece so that fish are
connected.)

2.   Sew on glass pebble beads for
eyes. Sew bugle beads randomly
over fish. ❧

euro pillow sham

MATERIALS

Euro pillow form: 26" square
Fabric for front and back: 2 yds.
Contrasting fabric for flange:
    1 $^1/_8$ yds.
Matching thread
Zipper: 22" long

GENERAL SUPPLIES

Scissors
Sewing machine
Straight pins

INSTRUCTIONS

1.   From front and back fabric,
cut one 27" square, one 26" x 27"
piece, and one 2" x 27" strip.

2.   Sew zipper to one long side of
the 2" strip; see Diagram A. Sew
strip to one long side of the 26" x
27" piece to make that piece
measure 27" square. This will be
the back.

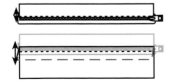

DIAGRAM A

3. From contrasting fabric, cut four 36" x 10" strips. Fold each strip in half lengthwise. Bring each corner down to the fold. Cut off corners and unfold.

4. Place two strips with right sides together and sew one corner; see Diagram B. Fold top strip back and sew third strip to other corner. Fold third strip back and sew last strip to corner. Bring ends together and sew last corner. (Note: You should now have a continuous square for flange; see Diagram C.) Clip corners and turn right side out. Press.

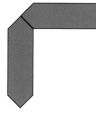

DIAGRAM B   **DIAGRAM C**

5. Pin flange around 27"-square piece of fabric, right sides together, with flange laying on the inside; see Diagram D. Unzip back piece slightly and place right side down on top of flange. Sew around all edges. Unzip zipper and turn sham right side out.

DIAGRAM D

6. Place pillow form inside pillow sham. ❧

fish pillow

MATERIALS

Fish panel (model used a
   13 ³/₄" x 8 ¹/₂" panel)
Fabric for pillow: 1 yd.
Contrasting fabric for cuff: ¹/₃ yd.
Buttons to cover: ⁷/₈" dia. (3)
Matching thread
Stuffing: 2 lbs.

GENERAL SUPPLIES

Scissors
Sewing machine
Sewing needle
Straight pins

INSTRUCTIONS

1. From pillow fabric, cut one piece 29" x 24 ¹/₂". From cuff fabric, cut one piece 10" x 29".

2. Place pillow fabric, right side up, on work surface with 24" edges at top and bottom. Cut out fish panel to measure 14" x 9" and center on bottom half of pillow fabric. Tuck edges of fish panel under ¹/₂" and secure with pins; top-stitch in place. Remove pins.

3. Fold top edge down to bottom edge. Sew a ¹/₂" seam across bottom. On right side edge, sew a seam 3" down from top and 3" up from bottom, leaving a 6" opening.

4. Bring 10" ends of cuff fabric together with right sides facing. Sew a seam. Fold cuff in half lengthwise with wrong sides together. Slip cuff into left side edge of pillow, matching bottom seam and placing raw edges together. Sew a seam down left edge through all layers. Turn right side out through 6" opening on right side edge.

5. Stuff pillow firmly and whipstitch opening closed.

6. Cover three buttons with pillow fabric and sew to cuff for decoration. ❧

fish quilt

MATERIALS

Fish panels: 9 (model used 17" x 9" panels)
Cotton fabrics: green plaid (3 yds.), dk. green print (3 yds.), red-checked (3 yds.)
Backing fabric: 60" wide (5 1/4 yds.)
Thin quilt batting
Thread: matching and transparent

GENERAL SUPPLIES

Scissors
Sewing machine
Sewing needle
Straight pins

INSTRUCTIONS

Finished size: 91" x 94"

1. From red-checked fabric, cut eleven 14" squares, four 3 1/2" x 17" pieces, one 14" x 17" piece, and two 3 1/2" x 14" pieces.

2. From green plaid fabric cut eleven 14" squares, two 14" x 17" pieces, and six 3 1/2" x 14" pieces.

3. From dark green print fabric, cut eleven 14" squares, two 14" x 17" pieces, and six 3 1/2" x 14" pieces.

4. Cut seven fish panels to measure 14" x 9" and two fish panels to measure 17" x 9". (Note: If fish panels are smaller than this, the strips used to sew onto panels will need to be adjusted.)

5. Using one large fish panel and two 3 1/2" x 17" strips of red-checked fabric, sew a strip along top and bottom of panel with a 1/2" seam. The finished panel should be 17" x 14". Repeat this step to make an additional panel.

6. Using small fish panel and two 3 1/2" x 14" strips of green plaid fabric, sew a strip along top and bottom of panel with a 1/2" seam. The finished panel should be 14" square. Repeat this step to make two additional panels.

7. Using small fish panel and two 3 1/2" x 14" strips of dark green print fabric, sew a strip along top and bottom of panel with a 1/2" seam. The finished panel should be 14" square. Repeat this step to make two additional panels.

8. Using small fish panel and two 3 1/2" x 14" strips of red-checked fabric, sew a strip along top and bottom of panel with a 1/2" seam. The finished panel should be 14" square.

9. Piece together the quilt one row at a time. The first row has larger blocks than the remaining rows. Refer to diagram (opposite page) as well as instructions. Pin together with a 1/2" seam.

First row: (All pieces should be pinned with long sides together) 17" x 14" red-checked fish (placed vertically with head up), 17" x 14" green plaid, 17" x 14" dark green print, 17" x 14" red-checked, 17" x 14" green plaid, 17" x 14" dark green print, 17" x 14" red-checked fish (head down).

Remaining rows use 14" squares.
Second row: dark green print, red-checked, green plaid, dark green print, red-checked, green plaid, dark green print.

Third row: green plaid fish (head up), dark green print, red-checked, green plaid, dark green print, red-checked, green plaid fish (head down).

Fourth row: red-checked, green plaid, dark green print, red-checked, green plaid, dark green print, red-checked.

Fifth row: dark green print fish (head up), red-checked, green plaid, dark green print, red-checked, green plaid, dark green print fish (head down).

Sixth row: green plaid, dark green print, red-checked, green plaid, dark green print, red-checked, green plaid.

Seventh row: skip first panel, green plaid fish (pointing left), dark green print, red-checked fish (pointing left), green plaid, dark green print fish (pointing left), skip panel.

10. Sew all panels of first row together. Sew remaining rows together. Press all rows.

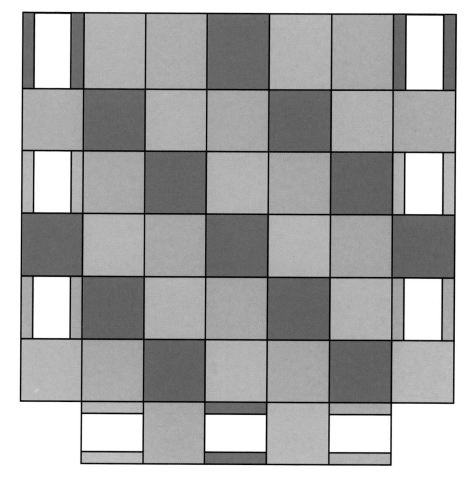

DIAGRAM

11. Pin first two rows together, matching the intersection of all squares. Sew together. Repeat with remaining rows.

12. Fold backing fabric in half with short edges matching; cut into two equal pieces. With edges of both pieces matching, sew together along one long edge to form backing for quilt. Trim to match quilt front. Use this as a pattern to cut batting.

13. Layer quilt back right side up, quilt front right side down, and batting on top. Pin in place. Sew around all edges with a $1/2$" seam, leaving a 24" opening at one end. Turn and stitch opening closed.

14. Pin at every intersection. Top-stitch around squares with transparent thread. Remove pins. ❧

STAND-UP SANTAS

MATERIALS

(For one Santa)

Fleece or fabric for body and arms: 1/3 yd.

Fleece or fabric for cap and mittens: 1/4 yd.

Fleece or felt for boots: 6" x 12"

Coordinating fabric scraps for embellishment

Lightweight fusible webbing: 1/2 yd.

Decorations: buttons, leather strips, small toys, and ribbon

Cardboard: 18" x 20"

GENERAL SUPPLIES

Clear tape
Craft knife
Glue: paper and fabric
Iron and ironing board
Ruler
Scissors
Tracing paper

INSTRUCTIONS

1. Enlarge patterns (below) 400%. From tracing paper, cut one body, one cap, boots, one ball for cap, one cap cuff, two arm cuffs, two arms, two mittens, one beard, and one of each mustache. Tape all pieces together to form Santa shape. (Note: If making more than one Santa, alternate directions of shapes for a different look.)

2. Place tracing paper Santa pattern onto cardboard. Trace outline of Santa shape. Using craft knife, cut shape from cardboard. Disassemble pattern pieces, removing tape.

3. Place patterns pieces, right side down, onto the right side of fusible webbing. Cut around patterns, leaving about 1/4" around pattern line.

4. Place fusible pattern pieces onto wrong side of desired fabrics and iron. Cut out exact pattern lines.

5. Iron onto cardboard shape in this order: boots, arms, body, cap, mittens, beard, mustache, ball on end of cap, cap cuff, and arm cuffs.

6. Referring to photograph, embellish Santa with buttons, leather, toys, and ribbon; secure with fabric glue.

To construct stand:

1. Enlarge stand pattern (below) 400%. Using craft knife, cut out stand from cardboard. Using a ruler and craft knife, score along one side of cardboard according to the marks on pattern. Do not score entirely through cardboard. Bend at score mark.

2. Glue thin cardboard strip to back of Santa with paper glue, allowing triangle portion to move freely; hold until set. ❧

ENLARGE PATTERNS 400%

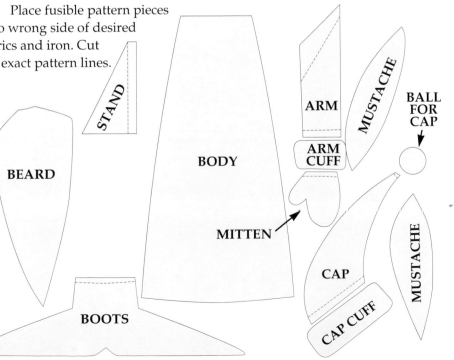

DECORATIVE STOCKINGS
(For decoration only)

MATERIALS

Stocking fabric: 24" x 16"
Coordinating fabric for toe, heel, and cuff: $1/4$ yd.
Fabric scraps for decorating (lettering, snowman, and stars)
Embellishments: buttons, raffia, and twigs
Lightweight fusible webbing: $1/2$ yd.
Poster board: 24" x 16"

GENERAL SUPPLIES

Fabric glue
Iron and ironing board
Paper punch
Scissors
Tracing paper

INSTRUCTIONS

1. Enlarge patterns (below) 400%. Cut out patterns from tracing paper.

2. Trace stocking shape onto poster board and cut out. Turn poster board pattern right side down and trace onto right side of fusible webbing. Cut around fusible pattern about 1" outside of pattern line.

3. Place fusible stocking pattern onto wrong side of stocking fabric. Iron lightly. Cut out exact stocking shape and place on poster board. Iron in place.

4. Place toe, heel, and cuff patterns right side down against right side of fusible webbing. Trace patterns and cut out shapes leaving about $1/2$" around pattern line. Iron patterns onto coordinating fabric and cut out exact shapes. Repeat for any fabric decorations (lettering, snowman, and stars). Make sure letters are traced onto fusible webbing in reverse so they will read correctly on stocking. Iron pieces onto stocking.

5. Adorn with buttons threaded with raffia. Glue twigs and buttons in place.

6. Tear several $1/2$"-wide strips from fabric scraps. Use a paper punch to make a hole in the top right corner below cuff. Thread fabric strips and raffia strands through hole, forming hanger. ❧

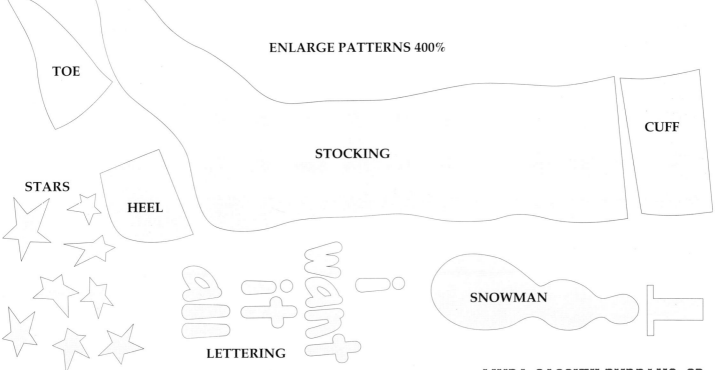

ENLARGE PATTERNS 400%

TOE

CUFF

STOCKING

STARS

HEEL

LETTERING

SNOWMAN

FESTIVE SALSA SERVERS

MATERIALS

Margarita glasses (or similar
    stemware): 3
Cinnamon sticks: 3" (6)
Dried cranberries: about 50
Natural twine
Twigs
Raffia
Ribbon: $1/4$" wide (6")

GENERAL SUPPLIES

Cardboard work surface: 5" x 18"
Craft glue
Craft knife
Large-eyed needle
Straight pins

INSTRUCTIONS

1. Cut twigs to 3" or to length of stem on glass.

2. Cut a 3" piece of ribbon and pin, centered horizontally, to cardboard. Run a thick bead of glue along ribbon. Center and line up twigs vertically across ribbon to measure 2 $1/2$". Let dry completely. Trim off excess ribbon. Remove pins from ribbon and lift twigs off cardboard.

3. Cut an 18" length of raffia. Center and glue raffia across twigs. Let dry completely.

4. Wrap twigs around stem of glass and crisscross raffia. Tie ends in a bow.

5. Repeat Steps 1 and 2 using cinnamon sticks.

6. Repeat Steps 3 and 4 using twine.

7. Cut a 50" length of twine. Thread needle and double the twine. Leaving a 9" tail, make a knot. Thread on dried cranberries for about 12". Tie 9" tail of the threaded cranberry strand to the bottom of the stem of the third glass. Wrap cranberry strand around stem, adding or subtracting cranberries to reach top of the stem on glass. Loosen wrap and make a knot at end of cranberries. Cut off twine, leaving a 9" tail at top. Wrap tightly again. Tie a bow with twine at top and bottom. ❧

(Note: Remove decorations before washing glasses.)

PHOTO ALBUM

MATERIALS

Three-ring binder (to accommodate
    8 $1/2$" x 11" pages)
Leather: 36" wide ($1/2$ yd.)
Fleece: coordinating ($1/2$ yd.)
Batting: 36" wide ($1/2$ yd.)
Conchos: silver (3)

GENERAL SUPPLIES

Fabric glue
Iron and ironing board
Pencil
Ruler
Scissors

INSTRUCTIONS

1. Lay leather on work surface with wrong side up. Place open binder on top of leather. Measure 1" from binder on all sizes and mark with pencil. Cut out leather.

2. Lay batting flat. Place binder on batting. Trace along edges of binder. Cut batting about $1/4$" inside tracing.

3. Glue batting to outside of binder using fabric glue. Allow to dry thoroughly.

4. Place batting side of binder onto wrong side of cut leather piece. Pull leather to the inside cover, trimming edges if necessary to get a smooth fold. Glue liberally in place. Hold until set.

5. Adorn front of cover with remaining leather scraps and conchos. To create fringe, cut leather in $1/4$" strips. Glue all pieces in place as desired.

6. Measure inside of front and back cover. Cut fleece to measure $3/4$" larger than each measurement.

7. Turn each fleece piece under 1" and press. Glue turned edges down. Glue fleece pieces to inside front and back of binder. ❧

TREE DOORS

MATERIALS

Wood stain
Wood (size and width will depend
    on finished size desired)
Copper sheeting (same size as wood)

GENERAL SUPPLIES

Glue (type to bond wood to metal)
Paintbrush
Sandpaper
Saw
Tin snips
Wood glue

INSTRUCTIONS

1. Enlarge tree pattern (right) to desired size. From wood, cut out one tree. Sand edges.

2. Using wooden tree as a pattern, trace onto copper sheeting and cut out about $1/8$" outside of pattern line.

3. Stain trees as desired.

4. Glue copper tree behind wood tree with appropriate adhesive. Let dry completely.

5. Glue trees to center of door with wood glue. (Note: Remove door from hinges and lay flat.) Allow glue to set before rehanging. ❧

**ENLARGE PATTERN
TO DESIRED SIZE**

TWIG TREES

MATERIALS

Assorted straight sticks: 9" long
Twine

GENERAL SUPPLIES

Craft knife
Hot glue gun and glue sticks
Large-eyed needle

INSTRUCTIONS

1. Referring to diagram (below), place sticks in a tree shape, cutting as necessary. Place a dot of hot glue at each joint.

2. Using a needle threaded with twine, wrap around and through sticks, tying them together. ❧

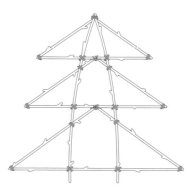

DIAGRAM

HARLEQUIN PRESENT PILLOW

MATERIALS

Satin fabric: cream ($^5/_8$ yd.)
Shimmering sheer fabric:
   cream ($^5/_8$ yd.)
Matching thread
Net ribbon: 3" wide, gold (3 $^1/_4$ yds.)
Stuffing: 24 oz.
Acrylic paints; all metallics: antique
   gold, gold, golden pearl, and
   med. gold
Textile medium
Glitter pen: gold
Sheet of dense craft foam: (used for
   stamping)

GENERAL SUPPLIES

Butcher paper (to cover work
   surface)
Paintbrushes: $^1/_2$" wide with stiff
   bristles (4)
Paper plates: 4
Scissors
Sewing machine
Sewing needle
Straight pins
Tape
Yardstick

INSTRUCTIONS

1.   Enlarge pattern (below) 200%. Trace pattern onto craft foam; cut four stamps. Be sure to leave tab on the corner for the stamp handle.

2.   Cover work surface with plain white paper. Tape down edges. Use yardstick to mark horizontal lines across the paper 4 $^1/_2$" apart, making six or seven rows.

3.   Place sheer fabric over paper, lining up top edge with first line. Tape corners of fabric to paper.

4.   Mix textile medium with paints following manufacturer's instructions, using one paper plate and paintbrush for each color of paint. Brush a light coat of paint on stamp, covering the bottom surface entirely except for tab and keeping

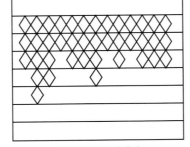

DIAGRAM A

ENLARGE PATTERN 200%

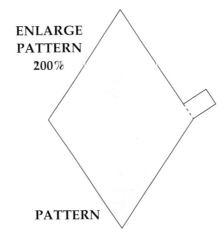

PATTERN

brush strokes in one direction. Begin stamping the fabric on top row, following the lines on the paper; see Diagram A. Alternate colors for each row, adding gold glitter as desired. Let dry completely.

5.   Cut stamped fabric 21 $^1/_2$" long x 30" wide. Cut satin same size. Place stamped fabric over satin fabric with right sides up. Zigzag around edges through both layers.

6.   Bring 21 $^1/_2$" sides together with right sides facing. Sew a seam 4" down from top and 4" up from bottom, leaving a 7" opening in the center.

7.   Center seam in middle and press open. Sew along top and bottom edges. Turn right side out and stuff firmly. Whipstitch opening closed.

8.   Cut an 18" length of ribbon and set aside. Fold remaining ribbon in half, end to end. Mark center with a pin.

9.   Place center of ribbon across bottom left corner; see Diagram B. Wrap under pillow and bring ends up at top right corner. Tie a bow with long tails.

10.   Loop tails back to center of bow and secure with a pin. Use 18" length of ribbon to tie overhand knot across all loops, securing bow. Remove pin, trim tails, and even out loops. ❧

DIAGRAM B

DIAMOND PILLOW

MATERIALS

Moire taffeta fabric: cream ($^5/_8$ yd.)
Wire-edge, mesh ribbon:
    $1^1/_2$" wide, gold (3 yds.)
Tassels: 4" long, cream (4)
Matching thread
Stuffing: 24 oz.

GENERAL SUPPLIES

Scissors
Sewing machine
Sewing needle

INSTRUCTIONS

1. Enlarge pattern (right) 400%. Cut two from taffeta.

2. Place pieces right sides together and sew $^1/_2$" seams around all edges, leaving a 5" opening.

3. Clip corners and turn right side out. Stuff corners first, then stuff rest of pillow snugly. Whipstitch opening closed.

4. Sew tassels to each corner. Wrap ribbon according to ribbon diagram (right). Tie all ribbon together in the center of pillow, arranging bow and tails. ❧

ALL WRAPPED UP PILLOW

MATERIALS

18"-square pillow
Nylon fabric: gold ($1^1/_4$ yds.)
Sheer, gold trimmed ribbon:
    $1^1/_2$" wide (4 yds.)
Large safety pins: 4

INSTRUCTIONS

1. Lay fabric out, wrong side up, and place pillow diagonally in the center of fabric; see wrapping diagram (below).

2. Pull opposite corners to center and wrap once, as if tying a knot. Pull ends until fabric is snug around center. Tuck ends inside and pin securely to pillow.

3. Repeat with other two corners. Reach inside of previous wraps to secure ends with safety pins. Adjust folds as needed.

4. Tie ribbon onto pillow according to wrapping diagram (below), wrapping across front to back, crisscrossing and coming back around to front. Tie a knot in center then tie bow. Trim ends as needed. ❧

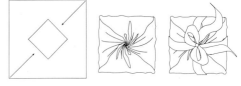

WRAPPING DIAGRAM

ENLARGE PATTERN 400%

Front   Back

RIBBON DIAGRAM

TERRESTRIAL CANDLEHOLDER

MATERIALS

Long-stemmed glasses
Acrylic paint: metallic gold
Glitter paint: gold
Paint pen: metallic gold
Texturizing medium

GENERAL SUPPLIES

Craft knife
Paintbrush
Plain paper
Scissors
Tape

INSTRUCTIONS

1.   Enlarge patterns (below) 400%. Trace star, moon, and sun shapes on plain paper. Cut shape out with craft knife, making a stencil.

2.   Tape stencil to glass. Use paint pen to draw shape onto glass. Fill in shape with pen.

3.   Mix small amount of texturizing medium into metallic gold paint. Paint over shapes on glass.

4.   When completely dry, paint shapes with gold glitter paint. Remove stencil. ❧

ENLARGE PATTERNS 400%

HARLEQUIN ORNAMENTS

MATERIALS

(For three ornaments)
Tassels: 3" long, cream (3)
Flat braid: $^1/_8$" wide, gold (1 $^1/_2$ yds.)
Acrylic paints: cream, lt. metallic gold, and med. metallic gold
Spray paint for fabric: antique gold
Acrylic matte spray sealer
Clear acrylic texturizing medium
Glitter pen: gold
Straight pins: $^1/_2$" long, gold (6)
Balsa wood: $^1/_8$" x 3" x 36"

GENERAL SUPPLIES

Craft knife
Paper towels
Ruler
Sandpaper
Toothpicks

INSTRUCTIONS

1.   Spray tassels with antique gold paint. Keep the tassel moving while spraying. Three or four coats may be needed to completely cover the tassel. Hang to dry.

2.   Enlarge pattern (below) 400%. Using a ruler to keep lines straight, cut out three ornaments from balsa wood with craft knife. Sand any rough edges.

3.   Enlarge stars, moon, and sun patterns (below, left) 400%. Transfer patterns onto fronts and backs of wood shapes.

4.   Use a toothpick to fill in design area with texturizing medium. Let dry completely.

5.   Paint around design with light metallic gold paint. Lightly wash same area with cream paint. Wipe off excess paint with paper towel.

6.   Paint design with medium metallic gold paint. Let dry completely.

7.   Apply gold glitter pen over design. Let dry. Spray ornaments with acrylic sealer.

8.   Cut ties from gold braid and secure to top of ornaments with straight pins. Attach tassels to bottom of ornaments with straight pins. ❧

ENLARGE PATTERN 400%

Gold Framed Mirrors

Materials

(For frame construction)
Pine board: 1" x 12" x 5

General supplies

(For frame construction)
Band clamp
Saw
Router
Sandpaper
Wood glue

Instructions

(For frame construction)
Finished size: 17 $^1/_2$" x 21"

1. Enlarge pattern (right) 400%. From 1" pine, cut out two frames.

2. Router inside of frame pieces to create a $^1/_4$"-wide groove along inside edge.

3. Glue the two frame halves together and secure with a band clamp. Let dry completely. Sand frame.

Materials

(For decorating frame)
Decorative trim: $^5/_8$" wide (4 yds.)
Scraps of trim and lace
Patterned netting: $^1/_2$ yd.
Spray paint: antique gold
Mirror: cut to fit inside finished
    frame
Frame: constructed using
    instructions above, or premade

General supplies

(For decorating frame)
Decoupage glue
Masking tape
Paintbrush: 2" wide
Straight pins

Instructions

(For decorating frame)
1. Spray frame with antique gold spray paint.

2. Using frame as a pattern, cut one from patterned netting. Place on top side of frame. Use straight pins to hold netting in place. (Note: The more pins used the better.)

3. Pin decorative trim around inside and outside of frame. Cut out pieces of lace and trim; arrange as desired on frame.

4. Brush decoupage glue over front of frame. Let dry completely. Spray entire frame again with antique gold spray paint. Let dry.

5. Secure mirror to back of frame with masking tape along routered edge. ❧

(Note: A staple gun and staples or small framing nails can be substituted for tape to hold mirror in place.)

**ENLARGE
PATTERN 400%**

charm picture frame

M ATERIALS

Acrylic paints: desired colors
Acrylic gloss spray sealer
Spray paint: antique gold
Assorted brass charms and buttons
    (50's motif, cars, bowling pins,
    Christmas items)
Assorted cola miniatures
Wood: $3/4$" x 6" x 5"
Eye screws: $1/2$" long (2)
Fine gold wire (for hanging)

G ENERAL SUPPLIES

Awl
Hammer
Industrial-strength glue
Masking tape
Paintbrushes
Sandpaper
Saw
Wire cutters

I NSTRUCTIONS

1. Enlarge desired frame pattern (right) 200%. Trace pattern onto wood and cut out. (Note: A purchased unfinished frame of this size may be substituted.) Sand frame until smooth. Spray frame with antique gold paint and let dry.

2. If necessary, cut off the backs of any buttons with wire cutters. Paint some of the charms and buttons as desired.

3. Cover entire front of frame with buttons and charms by gluing in place and overlapping as desired.

4. Spray frame with acrylic sealer.

5. With awl, make a hole on each side of top. Insert eye screws into holes. Tie a length of fine gold wire through eye screws for hanging.

6. Mount photo to back of frame with masking tape. ❧

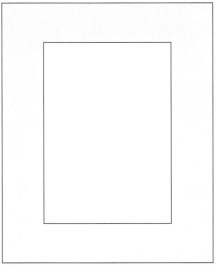

ENLARGE PATTERNS 200%

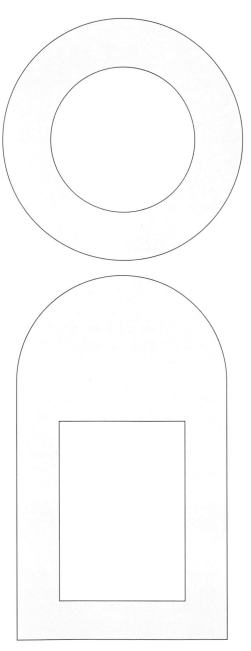

record frame

MATERIALS

Acrylic paints: black, lt. gold, lt. gray
Acrylic gloss spray sealer
Brass charms: bowling pins, car,
    poodle (or other assorted charms)
Miniature cola bottles: 2
Wood: $3/4$" x 6" x 6"
Eye screws: $1/2$" long (2)
Fine gold wire (for hanging)

GENERAL SUPPLIES

Awl
Hammer
Industrial-strength glue
Masking tape
Paintbrushes
Sandpaper
Saw
Wire cutters

INSTRUCTIONS

1. Enlarge circular frame pattern
(opposite page) 200%. Transfer
pattern onto wood and cut out.
Sand frame until smooth. Paint
frame black and let dry.

2. With slightly thinned light
gray paint, paint curved lines
around frame to resemble record
grooves. Paint a circle around
inside of frame with slightly
thinned light gold paint. Paint
several musical notes around frame.
When dry, spray with acrylic sealer.
Glue charms and miniatures at
random.

3. Follow Step 5 and Step 6 of
Charm Picture Frames (opposite
page) to complete frame. ❧

checkerboard frame

MATERIALS

Unfinished wood frame (model is
    26" x 30" with a 3"-wide border)
Enamel or tin cola sign (model is
    10" x 7")
Small cola bottles: 2
Acrylic paints: black, red, white
Acrylic gloss spray sealer
Wood strip: $1/4$" x 1$1/2$" (18" long)
Saw-tooth hanger with nails

GENERAL SUPPLIES

Drafting tape: $1/4$" wide
Hammer
Industrial-strength glue
Stiff paintbrush

INSTRUCTIONS

1. Tape off half of frame border
and paint inside red. Let dry
completely. Remove tape. Place
tape over red edge and paint other
half of frame border white. Let dry
completely. Remove tape.

2. Place tape in a checkerboard
pattern over white portion of frame.
Using paint sparingly, dab black
paint into uncovered squares; see
diagram. Let dry completely.
Remove tape. Spray with acrylic
sealer.

3. Cut 18" wood strip in half.
Turn frame over. Place sign in
desired position across top of
frame. Place wood strip on each
side of sign back so that it extends
across both the frame and the sign.
Glue in place with industrial-
strength glue.

4. Hammer sawtooth hanger
between wood strips on back of
frame.

5. Turn frame over and attach
small cola bottles to each side of
sign with industrial-strength glue. ❧

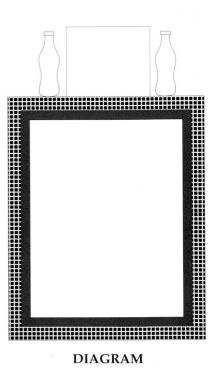

DIAGRAM

bear's party

MATERIALS

10" plush polar bears: 8
Miniature decorating accessories:
    bells, broom, cola glasses,
    cookies, hats, lights, and
    pom-poms
Assorted scraps: elastic, fabrics, lace
Acrylic paint: red
Spray paint: silver
Acrylic high-gloss spray sealer
Plywood: $^1/_4$" x 36" x 60"
Wood dowels: $^1/_2$" x 36" (1),
    $^3/_8$" x 4' (3)

GENERAL SUPPLIES

Band saw
C-clamps
Drill with $^3/_8$" and $^1/_2$" drill bits
Hammer
Hot glue gun and glue sticks
Paintbrushes
Sandpaper
Sewing needle
Wood glue

INSTRUCTIONS

1. Enlarge patterns (below) 200%. Trace patterns onto wood. Using band saw, cut out three table tops; also cut eight chair backs, 16 chair seat bottoms, and eight chair seat tops. Sand all edges to a smooth round edge.

2. From $^1/_2$"-diameter dowel, cut four 7" pieces. From $^3/_8$"-diameter dowels, cut 16 pieces 5"-long, and 32 pieces 4 $^1/_2$"-long.

3. Glue two table tops together with wood glue. Secure with clamps and let dry completely. Mark drill holes for leg placement. Drill with $^1/_2$" bit through both layers. Glue the 7" dowels up through holes in bottom of table, pushing through until flush with top. Spray paint legs and table base silver. Paint third table top red. Let dry. Glue red table top onto silver table base.

4. For each chair, glue two chair seat bottoms together. Clamp until dry. Mark drill holes for leg placement. Drill four $^3/_8$" holes through both layers of wood. Mark rail placement on chair seat top. Drill two $^3/_8$" holes through seat. Glue 4 $^1/_2$" dowels up through holes in bottom of chair. Paint chair base, legs, and back rails (5" dowels) silver. Paint seat top and chair back red. When dry, glue red seat to top of silver chair base. Insert back rails into holes in chair seat, lightly hammering if necessary. Tip chair onto its back and glue chair back to rails. Let dry. Spray table and chairs with acrylic sealer.

5. Dress bears, hot-gluing miniatures and accessories in place as desired. ❧

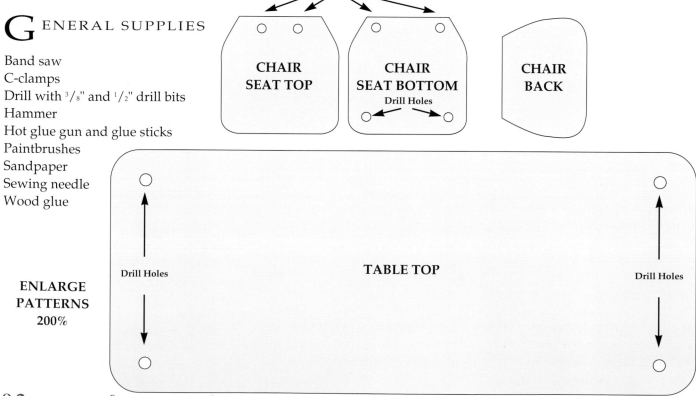

ENLARGE
PATTERNS
200%

Drill Holes

CHAIR
SEAT TOP

CHAIR
SEAT BOTTOM

Drill Holes

CHAIR
BACK

Drill Holes

TABLE TOP

Drill Holes

shower curtain

MATERIALS

Cotton shower curtain: white
Sheet of dense craft foam (used for
    stamping)
Acrylic paints: aqua, blue, lt. blue,
    cream, green, lavender, orange,
    pink, hot-pink, purple, red,
    yellow, and lt. yellow
Permanent marker, fine-point: black

GENERAL SUPPLIES

Iron and ironing board
Paintbrushes
Scissors
Terry cloth towel

INSTRUCTIONS

1. Enlarge patterns (right) 400%.
Transfer patterns to foam; cut out.
Be sure to leave tabs for the stamp
handles.

2. Coat foam shapes with
desired color of paint. Test on paper
until desired look is achieved. Start
with glasses first, stamping
randomly across shower curtain.

Press stamps firmly onto surface,
applying even pressure over entire
stamp. Lift off carefully to avoid
smearing. When changing color of
stamp, rinse and dry foam
thoroughly.

3. With paintbrush, swirl cream
paint around tops of each glass to
resemble soda foam. Let dry.

4. Stamp cherries, straws, and
candy canes in place. When coating
candy cane stamp, paint stripes
instead of covering the entire
surface.

5. Use black marker to draw
cord for lights. Add wording along
cord lines as desired.

6. Stamp lights along cord.

7. Use black marker to outline
and add detail to all shapes.

8. Place terry cloth towel over
shower curtain and set paint by
applying a hot iron. ❧

ENLARGE PATTERNS 400%

bath wreath

MATERIALS

Artificial wreath
Indoor miniature Christmas lights
Ribbon: 6 yds.
Decorations: bath beads, bottles of
    perfume, and colorful empty
    boxes
Plastic soda glass
Spray snow
Shredded paper
Scented spray or oil
Florist's wire

GENERAL SUPPLIES

Hot glue gun and glue sticks

INSTRUCTIONS

1. Wrap lights around wreath,
wiring in place if necessary.

2. Place plastic soda glass at base
of wreath and hot-glue. Glue
decorations randomly to wreath.
Fill soda glass with shredded
paper. Spray entire wreath lightly
with snow. Apply a heavier coat on
areas that are mainly green.

3. Tie ribbon into a multi-layered
bow and hot-glue in place. Spray
wreath daily with scented spray or
oil to freshen bathroom. ❧

Father Christmas

M ATERIALS

Santa head
Velvet coat; green
Gold braid
Sheep's wool for beard, hair, and brows
Artificial rabbit fur
Matching thread
Embellishments: beads, berries, buttons, old jewelry
Small grapevine wreath
Birthday candles
Spray paint: gold
Wood stain

G ENERAL SUPPLIES

Hot glue gun and glue sticks
Scissors
Sewing machine
Sewing needle

I NSTRUCTIONS

1. Remove beard and hair from Santa head. Antique the face by wiping on a small amount of wood stain. Hot-glue sheep's wool in place for beard, hair, and eyebrows.

2. Spray several candles with gold paint and let dry. Using wreath as a crown, glue candles in place at front. Add berries or other embellishments to crown as desired. Glue in place on Santa's head.

3. Trim velvet coat with artificial rabbit fur. Embellish with gold braid and any other decorations as desired. ❧

Candy House

M ATERIALS

Heavy cardboard
Plastic lens sheets
Artificial pine trees
Small Christmas lights: 1 string
Decorating candy: cinnamon candies, gumdrops, peppermint sticks
Rock candy
Graham crackers
Royal icing (recipe on opposite page)
Food coloring
Pastry bags with decorating tips

G ENERAL SUPPLIES

Craft knife
Hacksaw blade
Masking tape
Scissors
Spatula

I NSTRUCTIONS

1. Enlarge pattern (opposite page) to desired size. Model is 26" x 25" x 15". Size pattern so that the finished house fits your decorating

needs. From heavy cardboard, cut out pieces with craft knife or scissors. Cut out windows and door as desired.

2. Assemble house, using masking tape where each edge joins. Be generous with the tape and do not worry about the appearance, as it will be covered with icing.

3. Cut a piece of cardboard about 6" larger all around than house to use for base. Cut a hole in center of cardboard large enough for a hand to fit through.

4. Break pieces of plastic lens to fit behind windows. Masking tape in place.

5. Make royal icing. Use food coloring as desired. Model has white roof and tan sides. Place house on cardboard base. Spread icing liberally onto house with spatula, working small sections at a time. Cut rock candy in half with scissors and press into wet icing.

6. For even, unbroken shingles, cut graham crackers with hacksaw blade. Cover roof with icing and press shingles in place, overlapping as in photo (opposite page).

7. Place white icing in pastry bag and squeeze around roof top, forming snow. Add dark food coloring to icing and outline door, windows, and designs.

8. Decorate house with additional candy as desired.

9. Spread white icing over cardboard base. Place pine trees into the icing as desired. Press a peppermint stick path in front of door.

10. After icing has set, insert Christmas lights up through hole in cardboard base. Masking tape lights around inside of house. Tape light cord along underside of base around the back of the house. Plug in lights. ❧

(Note: Houses can last for years if carefully handled. Experiment with different shapes and sizes of houses, adding to your collection each year. Try a quaint Victorian house, or a tall, thin townhouse. Look at a photograph or drawing of the house you desire, picture it made of candy, and start creating.)

ROYAL ICING

4 cups sifted powdered sugar
3 Tbsp. meringue powder
6 Tbsp. water

In a medium mixing bowl, beat all ingredients with an electric mixer for seven minutes or until stiff peaks form. Reserve some of the icing for snow-covered roof. Tint remaining icing with desired food coloring. Cover icing with damp cloth to keep it from forming a crust when exposed to air. Keep tips that are in filled pastry bags tucked into damp paper towels. ❧

ENLARGE PATTERNS TO DESIRED SIZE

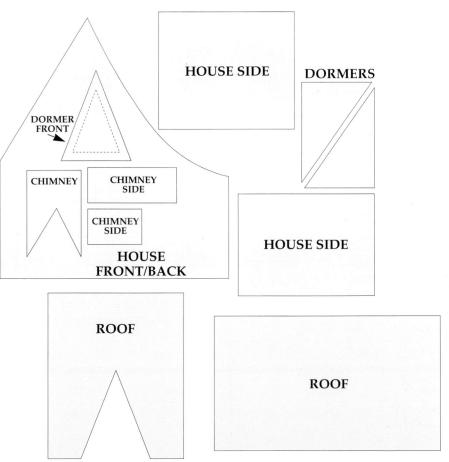

Paper Flowers

Materials

Flat fold crepe paper
Florist's wire

General supplies

Pencil
Scissors

Instructions

1.   Cut crepe paper into three sections as in diagram (below). If flowers are to be different sizes, cut each section a different width.

2.   Unroll one section of crepe paper. Roll one long edge around pencil one time, pushing, pulling, and twisting paper. This edge will stretch and stay in rolled position when pencil is removed. Roll and gather other long edge and secure with wire. Repeat for other flowers.

3.   Display flowers placed closely against trunk of Christmas tree. ❧

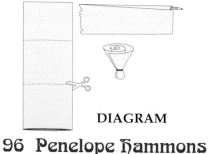

DIAGRAM

Santa Hat

Materials

Fabric for hat: $1/4$ yd.
Fur scrap for hat band
Matching thread
Jingle bell
Craft wire: 12 gauge

General supplies

Needle-nose pliers
Paper
Scissors
Sewing machine
Sewing needle

Instructions

1.   Determine the circumference of the head on which the hat will sit. Add $1 1/4$" to this measurement. This will be the length needed for the band. For the hat band width,

cut the desired size plus $1/2$". For example: For a head with a 14" circumference and a $1 1/2$" hat band, fur should be cut $15 1/4$" x 2". Once size has been determined, cut one from fur.

2.   Divide the length of the hat band by two. This will determine the width of the base of the triangle. The height of the triangle will depend upon desired finished size. For example: For an 18" long hat with same circumference as Step 1, make a triangle pattern with a base (short side) of $7 5/8$" and two 18" long sides. Cut two triangle patterns from hat fabric.

3.   Place both fabric triangles with right sides together. Zigzag along both long edges. Sew a seam $1/8$" in from one long edge. Next to this seam, sew a casing $1/4$" wide. Sew a $1/4$" seam along remaining long edge.

4.   Bring short edges of hat band with right sides together and sew a $1/2$" seam. Turn hat right side out and slip hat band over base of hat so that right sides are together and raw edges are aligned. Sew a $1/2$" seam around hat and hat band, leaving a $1/4$" opening at the casing. Fold hat band down.

5.   Cut an 18" length of wire. Bend one tip of wire with pliers and thread that tip through casing. Tack to top of hat with needle and thread. Bend other tip of wire and pull down to bottom of hat band. Tack in place. Hat can now be gathered, bent, and twisted as desired.

6.   Sew bell on tip of hat. ❧

Three Dried Trees

MATERIALS

Clay pots with saucers: 3
Assorted strong dried weeds, boughs, and thistles with sturdy bases
Decorations: berries, dried flowers, small ornaments, and pine cones
Dried moss
Florist's foam: 3 blocks
Spray paint: gold

GENERAL SUPPLIES

Hot glue gun and glue sticks (if desired)

INSTRUCTIONS

1. Insert a block of florist's foam into each pot; cover with dried moss.

2. Spray strong weeds gold and let dry. Insert one into center of each pot, making sure it is evenly balanced and weighted. (Note: You may have to add other weights inside the flower pot to make the arrangement sturdy enough to support decorated trees.)

3. Decorate with flowers, berries, pine cones, and small ornaments. Decorations need not be glued on, but can be if desired. 🍂

Bark Tree

MATERIALS

Styrofoam cone, large
Bark and other natural materials
Pearl garland and desired decorations
Spray paint: gold or brown

GENERAL SUPPLIES

Hot glue gun and glue sticks

INSTRUCTIONS

1. Cover cone completely with gold or brown spray paint.

2. Starting at the bottom, glue bark pieces to cone, working around base and then up, overlapping to give a tree branch effect.

3. Decorate tree with pearl garland or any sort of beads, berries, or cones. 🍂

Basket Centerpiece

MATERIALS

Rustic basket
Styrofoam balls
Berries, willow buds, dried flowers, and fruits—real or artificial
Pine sprigs
Ornaments, pine cones, and leaves
Spray paint: brown or gold

GENERAL SUPPLIES

Hot glue gun and glue sticks

INSTRUCTIONS

1. Cover balls completely with brown or gold spray paint.

2. Hot-glue assorted berries or flowers, covering balls.

3. Arrange decorated balls in basket with ornaments, pine cones, and leaves. Place basket on a bed of pine sprigs. 🍂

Willow Wreath

Materials

Baling wire (or purchased wreath
     form)
Willow branches
Dried flowers: statice, baby's
     breath, or other denser material
     for inner wreath
Decorations: berries, fruit, pine
     cones, and ribbons

General Supplies

Hot glue gun and glue sticks

Instructions

1.   Form wreath shape out of wire.
Begin to weave willow branches into
wire form, starting in one place and
working around the perimeter so
that all branches emerge at the same
approximate angle.

2.   Using statice, or other desired
material, form inner wreath, hiding
any visible wire.

3.   Decorate as desired, hot gluing
decorative items if needed. ❧

(Note: Wreath can be made to go
around clock or door, or use as a
wall hanging by itself. Adjust size
accordingly.)

Formal Centerpiece

Materials

Unique container (model used iron
     melting pot)
Dried roses, leaves, and filler
     (statice or baby's breath)
Pepper berries
Dried moss
Ornaments as desired
Florist's foam

General Supplies

Hot glue gun and glue sticks (if
     desired)

Instructions

1.   Place florist's foam in
container; cover with dried moss.

2.   Start to build arrangement,
beginning with the filler. Add dried
leaves or other dried materials for
added shape. Insert dried roses.
Decorations need not be glued on,
but can be if desired.

3.   Add pepper berries and any
other ornamentation desired. ❧

Hanging Ornaments

Materials

(For one ornament)
Freeze dried ferns or other leaves
Dried flowers
Artificial fruit or berries
Ribbon
Florist's wire

General Supplies

Hot glue gun and glue sticks (if
     desired)

Instructions

1.   Wire dried ferns or leaves,
flowers, and fruit or berries
together as desired so that the base
is at the top and the materials hang
downward.

2.   Tie a large bow and attach to
top of arrangement, covering wire.
Bow need not be glued on, but can
be if desired. ❧

Moss Ornament

MATERIALS

Styrofoam ball
Dried moss
Ribbon for hanger
Assorted decorations: berries, dried
    or silk flowers, greenery, pine
    cones, and pods

GENERAL SUPPLIES

Craft glue
Hot glue gun and glue sticks

INSTRUCTIONS

1. Cover foam ball with craft glue and press moss into place.

2. Hot-glue ribbon to top of ball for hanger. Arrange and glue decorations to top of ornament as desired. ❧

Fruit Basket

MATERIALS

Small basket
Artificial fruit, flowers, and leaves
Styrofoam form to fit basket
Dried moss
Plastic spray
Wood stain

GENERAL SUPPLIES

Hot glue gun and glue sticks
Old paintbrush

INSTRUCTIONS

1. Lightly brush stain over fruit to give antique look. Let dry.

2. Glue foam into basket. Arrange fruit, flowers, and leaves around foam, gluing in place. Place moss in any openings and around base.

3. Spray contents of basket with plastic spray. ❧

Waxed Ornaments

MATERIALS

(For 10–12 medium ornaments)
Plastic fruit forms with stems
Paraffin wax: 2 blocks
Ribbons for ornament hangers
Assorted decorations: berries, dried
    or silk flowers, greenery, pine
    cones, and pods
Glitter spray: desired color

GENERAL SUPPLIES

Aluminum foil
Hot glue gun and glue sticks
Paintbrush
Pans: large ($10 \frac{1}{2}$" dia.),
    small ($6 \frac{1}{2}$" dia.)

INSTRUCTIONS

1. Fill large pan with $2 \frac{1}{2}$" of water and bring to a boil. Turn setting to low. Place blocks of wax into smaller pan. Place smaller pan inside of large pan and let wax melt. (Note: Wax is flammable and should not be left unattended.)

2. Place a sheet of foil onto work surface. Hold fruit forms by the stems over pan and paint wax on with brush. Place onto foil and let dry. Repeat for other pieces. (Note: If wax builds up too much in a certain area, simply cut away and wax that portion again.)

3. Hot-glue ribbon to top of fruit for hanger. Arrange and glue decorations to top of fruit as desired. Spray lightly with glitter. ❧

Cinderella's Coach Ornament

MATERIALS

Pumpkins: Styrofoam or plastic, 4" dia. (1), 1" dia. (1)
Small stuffed person (for coachman, optional)
Decorative trim: 1 yd.
Lace: 7"
Thin wired cording: silver (12")
Thread: silver
Vine greenery
Acrylic paint: desired colors (model used shades of blue, silver, and white)
Acrylic matte spray sealer
Spray paint: white and silver
Spray adhesive
Wooden oval: 5 3/4" x 3 3/4"
Spoked wheels: 1 3/4" dia. (4)

GENERAL SUPPLIES

Hot glue gun and glue sticks
Paintbrushes
Pencil

INSTRUCTIONS

1. Spray large pumpkin with a base coat of white paint. (Note: If pumpkin is plastic, coat first with spray adhesive. This will provide a better surface for paint to adhere to. When using spray adhesive as a bonding agent, hold object about 18" away and spray very lightly.)

2. Enlarge desired pattern (opposite page) 175%. Lightly transfer pattern onto large pumpkin. Paint large pumpkin following pattern or as desired. Paint small pumpkin as desired. Spray with acrylic sealer.

3. Glue trim on for windows. Glue lace to top of windows for curtains.

4. Spray paint vine silver. When dry, glue vine to top of larger pumpkin. Curl wired cording around a pencil and glue next to vine.

5. Make a hole in bottom of small pumpkin to fit over larger pumpkin's stem. Glue small pumpkin in place. Glue on stuffed coachman if desired.

6. For base, paint top of wooden oval white. Paint sides and bottom in desired color combination. Glue trim around sides of base.

7. Paint wheels and let dry. Glue wheels to base. Spray base with acrylic sealer. Glue pumpkin coach onto base; see diagram.

8. Hang from tree with silver thread. ❧

DIAGRAM

ENLARGE PATTERNS 175%

Cinderella's Tree Skirt

MATERIALS

Cotton batiste fabric: white
  (8 1/4 yds.)
Lace for first layer: crocheted
  (12 1/2 yds.)
Lace for second layer: 1/2" wide
  (10 yds.); 7/8" wide (10 yds.);
  5/8" wide insertion (10 yds.);
  5" wide (9 yds.)
Lace for third layer: 1 1/4" wide
  insertion (10 yds.); 2" wide
  insertion (5 yds.); 1/2" wide
  (5 yds.)
Lace around top: 1 1/2" (45")
Satin ribbon: 1/4" wide (10 yds.);
  1/2" wide (5 yds.)
Thin cording: 45"
Matching thread

GENERAL SUPPLIES

Iron and ironing board
Measuring tape
Scissors
Sewing machine
Straight pins

INSTRUCTIONS

1.   For layer one (bottom), cut two 30"-wide half circles from batiste. Sew together halfway to center to make a 60"-diameter circle with a slit to middle. For layer two (middle), cut two 25"-wide half circles from batiste. Sew together halfway to center to make a 50"-diameter circle with a slit to middle. For layer three (top), cut a 26" circle from batiste and cut a slit from edge to center. Set layers aside.

2.   For first layer ruffle, cut ten strips from batiste, each 45" x 4". Sew together along the short edges to form one long strip. Sew a gathering thread across top edge of strip. Set aside.

3.   For second layer ruffle, cut eight strips from batiste, each 45" x 9". Sew as in Step 2.

4.   For third layer ruffle, cut four strips from batiste, each 45" x 10". Sew as in Step 2.

5.   Starting 2" down from the top edge of first ruffle, sew three rows of pin tucks 1/4" apart, using a double needle and the presser foot as a guide. Roll hem bottom edge. Sew crocheted lace around bottom. Pull top gathering thread and pin ruffle around 60" circle, starting and ending at the slit. Stitch in place.

6.   Press and sew a 2" hem along bottom edge of second ruffle. Pin 1/4"-wide ribbon around front of ruffle at hem mark. Pin 1/2"-wide lace over ribbon. Stitch in place. Measure up 3" from bottom of hem and press a 3/8" tuck. Stitch in place. Measure up 1 1/4" from tuck and sew top edge of 7/8" lace around ruffle. Measure up 1" from previous lace and sew 5/8" insertion lace around ruffle; see note on opposite page. Pull top gathering thread and pin ruffle around 50" circle, starting and ending at the slit. Stitch in place. Measure up 4" from top of ruffle and sew a 5"-wide lace ruffle around circle.

7. Sew 1 1/4"-wide insertion lace vertically across the third ruffle every 5". Weave the 1/2"-wide ribbon through the 2"-wide insertion lace. Sew the woven insertion lace 3" up from the bottom of ruffle; see note below. Serge bottom hem of ruffle. Stitch 1/2"-wide lace around hem. Pull top gathering thread and pin ruffle around 26" circle, starting and ending at the slit. Stitch in place.

8. Hem raw edges of the slits, catching both ruffle and circle in hem. Layer the circles right side up from the largest to the smallest, matching slits. Sew circles together, still keeping the slit open. Measure and cut a 10"-diameter circle in center of skirt through all layers.

9. Cut a 3" bias strip from batiste. Press in half lengthwise with wrong sides together. Pin raw edges of bias strip around raw edges of cut-out circle on skirt. Sew a 5/8" seam. Sew 1 1/2"-wide lace along seam line. Insert cording inside of strip against the fold. Sew a narrow casing to hold cording. ❧

(Note: To finish the insertion lace, sew down both sides of lace with a straight stitch. Cut down the middle of the underneath fabric and press open. Turn back to right side and sew a small zigzag-stitch down both sides of lace. Carefully trim away excess fabric from under side. This step can be done immediately after stitching the insertion lace, or after the entire project is finished.)

Slipper Ornaments

MATERIALS

(For one ornament)
Clear plastic slipper: between 3"– 4" long
Miscellaneous embellishments: beads, birds, braid, buttons, charms, flowers, lace, ribbons, and tassels
Fabric scraps: satin, silk, taffeta, or velvet (two 5" x 6" pieces)
Thread: silver
Stuffing

GENERAL SUPPLIES

Drill with 1/16" drill bit
Industrial-strength adhesive
Sewing machine
Toothpicks

INSTRUCTIONS

1. Use toothpick to apply glue to toe of slipper. Embellish as desired.

2. For cushion, cut two 5" x 6" rectangles. Stitch desired trim (braid, tassels, and lace) around edge of one rectangle. Trim should be placed on the right side of fabric, pointing in to center. Place rectangles right sides together. Sew a 1/4" seam along edges leaving a 2" opening. Turn and stuff cushion. Whipstitch opening closed. Glue slipper to center of cushion.

3. To hang ornament on tree, drill a small hole in back of slipper's heel. Insert silver thread through hole to make hanger. ❧

Cuffed Stocking

Materials

Lining fabric: $^1/_2$ yd.
Organdy fabric: $^1/_2$ yd.
Taffeta fabric: $^1/_2$ yd.
Satin fabric: $^3/_8$ yd. (cuff trim)
Velvet fabric: $^1/_4$ yd. (cuff)
Ribbon: 12" (for hanging)
Matching thread
Buttons to cover: 2

General Supplies

Iron and ironing board
Scissors
Sewing machine
Straight pins

Instructions

1.   Enlarge patterns (opposite page) 400%. Cut two stockings each from taffeta, organdy and lining fabrics. Cut one cuff each from velvet and taffeta fabrics.

2.   Cut 2" bias strips from satin to make a 16 $^1/_2$" circle for cuff trim.

3.   Bring short ends of velvet cuff together and sew a seam. Repeat with taffeta cuff.

4.   Place satin band around bottom edge of taffeta cuff with right sides together; secure with pins. (Note: Position band so that the piecing seam will be on the back of the cuff. The seam on the cuff will be on the right side.) Sew band onto cuff with a $^3/_8$" seam; remove pins. Place other edge of band around bottom edge of velvet cuff, with right sides together, making sure cuff seams line up. Sew a $^3/_8$" seam. Fold cuff so that wrong sides are together and raw edges are at the top. Ditch-stitch between cuff and trim.

5.   Hand-stitch button holes (decorative) on right side of cuff front. Cover two buttons with satin and sew onto button holes.

6.   Place organdy stockings over taffeta stockings. Zigzag around edges and handle as one piece. Place front and back of stocking with organdy sides together. Stitch around stocking, leaving top open. Turn right side out; press.

7.   Place lining pieces right sides together. Sew around edges, leaving top open. Leave lining inside out. Insert lining into stocking. Place cuff into stocking with velvet side down. Sew around raw edges through all layers. Turn cuff out and fold down.

8.   Sew ribbon inside of stocking for hanger. ❧

Floral Stocking

MATERIALS

Lining fabric: ¹/₂ yd.
Organdy fabric: ¹/₂ yd.
Taffeta fabric: ¹/₂ yd.
Cheesecloth: 18"
Ribbon: 12" (for hanging)
Matching thread
Decorations: velvet and silk
    flowers, ribbons, and beads

GENERAL SUPPLIES

Iron and ironing board
Scissors
Sewing machine
Straight pins

INSTRUCTIONS

1. Assemble stocking as in
instructions for Cuffed Stocking on
opposite page, omitting the cuff.

2. Decorate with velvet and silk
flowers, beads, ribbons, and
cheesecloth draped underneath and
sewn into the seams. ❧

(Note: Cheesecloth may be shaped
by spraying with starch,
scrunching, and then letting dry.)

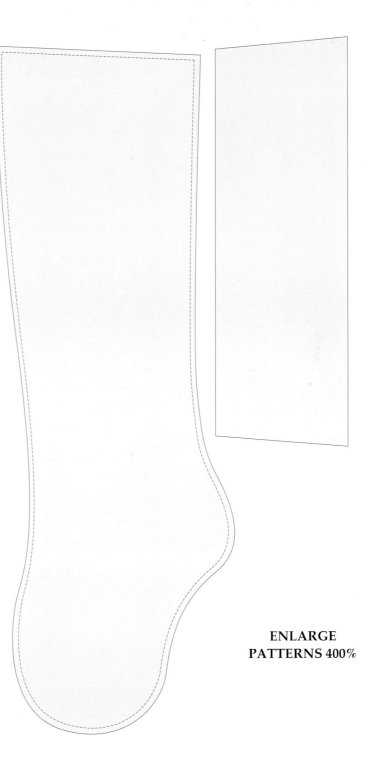

**ENLARGE
PATTERNS 400%**

Fairy Godmother Tree Top

MATERIALS

Muslin fabric: ¹/₄ yd.
Cotton organdy fabric: white
 (¹/₂ yd.)
Nylon organdy fabric: white
 (¹/₂ yd.)
Sheer fabric: shimmering white
 (⁵/₈ yd.)
Jacquard taffeta fabric: white
 (¹/₂ yd.)
Velvet fabric: blue (4" square)
Braid: ¹/₂" wide, metallic silver (1 yd.)
Lace: 3" wide, pointed (1 ¹/₂ yds.);
 1 ¹/₂" wide, silver (1 yd.);
 1" wide, cotton (1 yd.);
 ¹/₂" wide, silver edged (1 ¹/₄ yd.)
Dressmaker's pen
Silk ribbon, 4mm: lt. blue, med.
 blue, white
Stuffing: 12 oz.
Thread: white and heavy-duty
Seed beads: lt. blue
Flat-back jewels: round (19);
 marquee (1)
Acrylic paints: black, blue, lt. blue,
med. blue, pale blue, lt. peach,
 lt. pink, rose, and white
Fabric writer: silver glitter
Permanent marker, fine-point: black
Wooden dowel, ⁵/₈" wide: 4"
Cardboard cone: 7" tall with 2" base
Wire, 16 gauge: silver (24")

GENERAL SUPPLIES

Craft glue
Fray preventative
Hot glue gun and glue sticks
Iron and ironing board
Needle-nose pliers
Needles: beading and hand-sewing
Paintbrushes
Paper towels
Pencil
Scissors
Sewing machine
Straight pins

INSTRUCTIONS

1.   Enlarge patterns (page 108) 200%. Transfer patterns for head, body, and two arms onto wrong side of muslin fabric, transferring both solid and dotted lines. Place another piece of muslin directly under transferred patterns with right side up. Pin muslin pieces together and handle as one.

2.   Stitch around solid lines, leaving an opening for turning. (Note: Stitching the shape before cutting helps keep the correct shape and allows for easier handling.) Cut around the dotted lines. Clip curves and turn right side out. Stuff each piece firmly. The eraser end of a pencil will help ease stuffing into hard to reach spots. Whipstitch head and arms closed. Run a gathering thread around bottom edge of body. Insert the 4" piece of dowel into bottom of body and pull gathering threads tight. Apply glue to this area. Glue other end of dowel into top of cone, fitting snugly in place.

3.   Make a half and half mixture of light peach and light pink paint. Paint stuffed body, arms, and head. Let dry. With pencil, draw eyes and lips onto face. Use white paint to paint eyes. When completely dry, paint iris of eyes black. Use a small amount of blue and white paint to highlight irises. When completely dry, use silver glitter writer to paint pupil of eye. Paint lips with rose paint. When all paint is dry, outline lips and eyes, and draw eyelashes with black marker.

4.   Cover work surface with paper towels. Place nylon organdy flat. Using all shades of blue, and thinning with water, paint stripes blending colors together. Paint ¹/₂ yd. of the fabric. Go over stripes with silver glitter fabric writer; let dry.

5.   From painted fabric, cut two sleeves, one bodice front, two bodice backs, and a 12" x 36" piece for overskirt.

6.   From jacquard taffeta, cut two sleeves, two bodice fronts, four bodice backs, and a 12" x 36" piece for underskirt.

7.   From cotton organdy, cut a 11" x 36" piece for petticoat.

8.   From sheer fabric, cut two capes.

9.   From pointed lace, cut one 5" piece or five points. Cut one 8" piece or eight points.

10. Bring short edges of petticoat right sides together and sew a seam. Fold top edge over $1/2$" and sew a casing. Zigzag along bottom edge. Sew $1 1/2$"-wide silver lace along bottom edge. Now sew the 1"-wide cotton lace on top of previous lace. Next sew the $1/2$"-wide silver trimmed lace on top of other laces. Thread a length of heavy thread through casing. Slip petticoat over cone and pull thread tightly. Knot off.

11. Place cape pieces right sides together. Sew a $1/4$" seam around sides and bottom of cape. Clip curves well. Turn right side out. Carefully use a pin to pull points out. Fold pleats across top edge and sew as indicated on pattern. Press cape.

12. For collar, place 8" of 3"-wide pointed lace right side up on a scrap of organdy. Sew around edges of lace. Trim off excess fabric. Sew a row of light blue beads along points of lace about $1/4$" in from edge and following lace pattern. Run a gathering thread along the other edge. Pull thread until collar matches line of cape. Glue jewels on collar. Place collar around cape and pin in place. (Note: The edge of cape will not be even with the collar because of the pleats.) Use the collar as the sewing line. Sew along edge of collar through all thicknesses. Trim off any excess cape fabric. Zigzag along this edge.

13. Fold blue velvet in half with right sides together. Trace hat pattern onto velvet. Sew around solid lines through both thicknesses. Cut out hat. Clip curves and turn right side out. Use fray preventative along unfinished edges. From desired color of silk ribbon, cut two 4" lengths. Sew to each corner of hat

for ties. Place hat on doll head and tie ribbons under chin.

14. For dress bodice, layer painted bodice pieces with one set of taffeta pieces and treat as one piece by zigzagging edges together. Use a $1/4$" seam for assembly. Sew shoulder seams with right sides together. Repeat shoulder seams on other set of taffeta bodice pieces (lining). Place the layered bodice piece and the lining with right sides together. Sew up the back, around the neck, and down the back. Clip curves well and flip right side out. Press.

15. Layer painted sleeve pieces with taffeta pieces as above. Gather sleeves between dots and sew into arm holes. Fold bodice and sleeves, right sides together, and sew under arms and down side seams.

16. Hem one long edge of taffeta underskirt. On painted overskirt, sew $1/2$"-wide metallic silver braid and 3"-wide pointed lace along one long edge (bottom). Place overskirt on top of underskirt and sew two gathering threads across top. At this point, mark ribbon embroidery pattern along bottom of skirt according to pattern on page 109. Stitch ribbon work through both layers. Sew skirts together along back seam. Pull gathering threads around waist and sew to bodice with right sides together. Turn right side out.

17. With dressmaker's pen, transfer ribbon embroidery pattern (page 109) on bodice. Stitch design.

18. Slip dress onto doll and whipstitch back bodice to close.

19. For crown, place 5" piece of 3"-wide pointed lace, right side up, on a

scrap of organdy. Sew along edges and trim off extra fabric. Sew in darts and hand-sew silver trim to bottom edge. Glue on jewels and highlight with silver glitter fabric writer. Let dry. Tack together at back and place on head. Stitch in place.

20. Hand-sew cape in place on shoulders.

21. For wand, grasp end of wire with pliers and twist seven or eight times to form top ball. Bend two curves into wire just under the top. Paint wand as desired and highlight with glitter. Stitch wand to hand. ❧

E MBROIDERY
INSTRUCTIONS
Lazy Daisy Stitch
Bring needle up at A. Keep the ribbon flat, untwisted, and full. Put the needle down through fabric at B and up through fabric at C, keeping the ribbon under the needle to form a loop. Pull the ribbon through, leaving the loop loose and full. To hold the loop in place, go down on other side of ribbon near C, forming a straight stitch over loop.

DIAGRAM

Straight Stitch
Come up through fabric at A. Go down at B, keeping the ribbon flat.

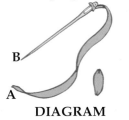

DIAGRAM

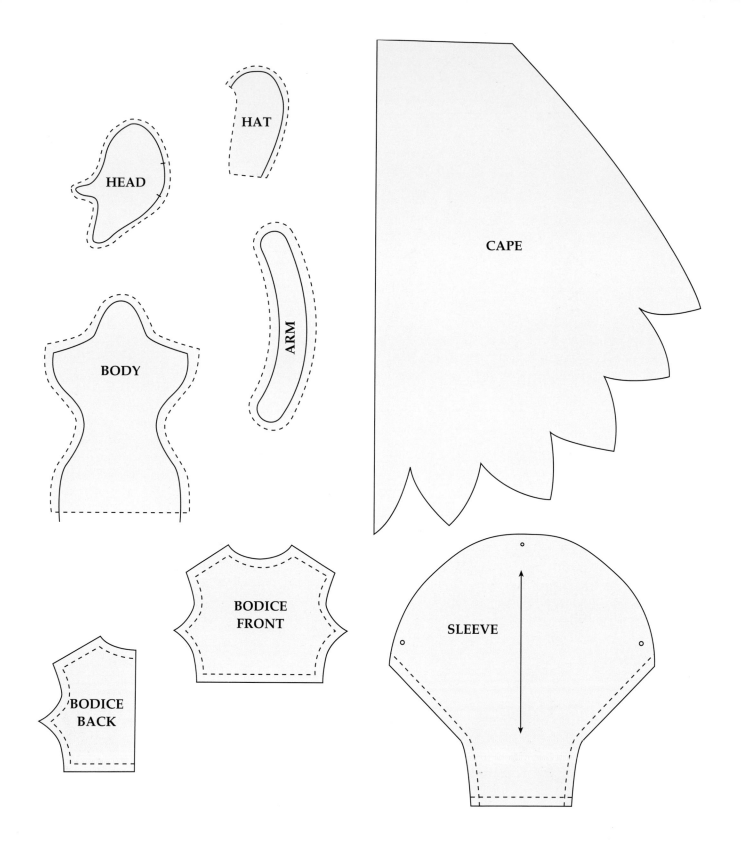

HEAD

HAT

CAPE

BODY

ARM

BODICE FRONT

SLEEVE

BODICE BACK

ENLARGE PATTERNS 200%

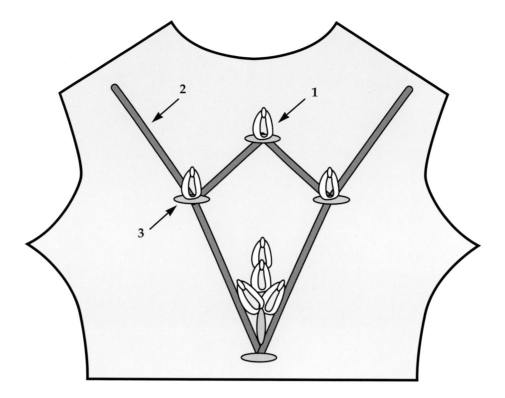

STITCH GUIDE

Item	#	Color	Stitch
Bud	1	White	Lazy Daisy Stitch
Long Lines	2	Med. Blue	Straight Stitch
Short Lines	3	Lt. Blue	Straight Stitch

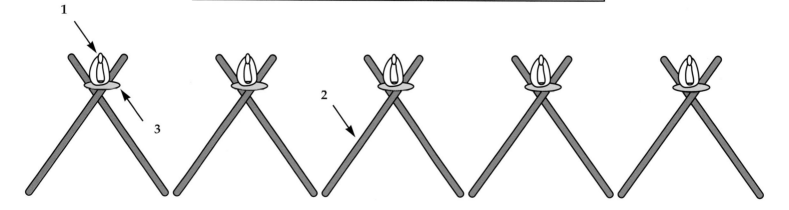

Coach Planters

MATERIALS

(For one planter)

Pumpkin: plastic Halloween candy container with handles removed (7 1/2" dia.)

Assorted decorations: charms, cording, beads, lace, ribbons, trims

Acrylic paint: desired colors (model used shades of blue, silver, and white)

Acrylic matte spray sealer

Primer spray

Spray adhesive

Wooden plaque: unfinished

Wooden wheels: 2 1/2" (4)

Wooden pegs, 1/4": 2 1/2" (4)

GENERAL SUPPLIES

Drill with 1/4" drill bit

Glue: Industrial-strength, tacky, and wood

Paintbrushes

INSTRUCTIONS

1. Spray pumpkin with spray adhesive. This will provide a better surface for paint to adhere to. (Note: When using spray adhesive as a bonding agent, hold object about 18" away and spray very lightly.)

2. Drill holes in sides of wood plaque for axles, referring to photo (above) for placement.

3. Enlarge desired pattern (right) 400%. Lightly transfer pattern onto pumpkin. Paint pumpkin following pattern or as desired. Paint wood plaque and wheels as desired or refer to photo (above). Spray with acrylic sealer.

4. Decorate pumpkin coach as desired, Use tacky glue to glue accessories on.

5. Place wood pegs in drill holes; secure with a small amount of wood glue. Glue wheels to axles with wood glue. Attach pumpkin to center of plaque with industrial-strength glue. ❧

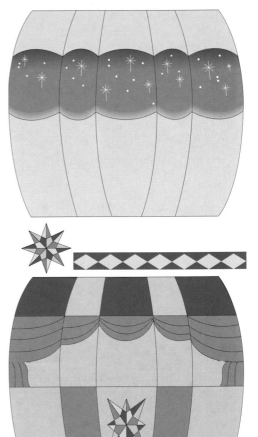

ENLARGE PATTERNS 400%

Pumpkin Ornaments

MATERIALS

(For one ornament)
Pumpkin: Styrofoam or plastic
　　(4" dia.)
Vine greenery
Florist's wire: green (12")
Medium wire: 6"
Thread: silver

GENERAL SUPPLIES

Hot glue gun and glue sticks
Pencil
Wire cutters

INSTRUCTIONS

1.　Cut medium wire in half. Fold both wires in half, twisting bottom ends and leaving a loop at the top. Cut off bottoms to $1/2$". Push a wire loop into pumpkin on each side of stem. Insert thread through loops to hang.

2.　Glue vine to top of pumpkin. Cut florist's wire in half. Wrap each piece around pencil to curl. Glue to top of pumpkin. ❧

Stick Bundles

MATERIALS

Twigs
Natural jute: 4-ply

GENERAL SUPPLIES

Craft knife
Scissors

INSTRUCTIONS

1.　Cut twigs into 8" lengths. Separate into bundles.

2.　Tie a knot in jute, leaving a loop at the top. Wrap ends around stick bundles twice. Secure and clip ends. ❧

Stick Star

MATERIALS

Assorted straight sticks: 9" long
Twine

GENERAL SUPPLIES

Craft knife
Hot glue gun and glue sticks
Large-eyed needle

INSTRUCTIONS

1.　Place five sticks in a star shape; see diagram (below). Place a dot of hot glue in corners.

2.　Use twine to tie corners together, wrapping twine around and through. Repeat for inside crosses; see diagram (below). ❧

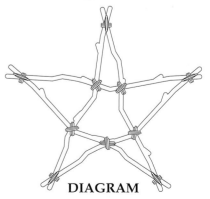

DIAGRAM

Run thumb over toothbrush and splatter paint onto surface. When dry, rub edges of painted wood with sandpaper. Spray project with acrylic sealer.

5. Cut cotton bias strip in half. Wrap tightly around mitten cookie cutter, gluing at beginning and end. Repeat for other mitten. Tie mittens together with twine. Tie knots along twine and glue stars to knots. Hang from twig arm.

6. Paint pail as desired. Model is painted dark gold with hunter green trim and a holly and berries design, and is sanded and washed in same manner as snowman. Make a bundle with thin twigs and tie with twine. Cut pine pick into pieces and glue into pail with twig bundle. Hang from twig arm.

7. Paint birdhouse as desired and hang from other twig arm.

8. Attach stand to back of snowman with wood glue. Stand snowman behind stocking holder. ❧

(Note: A Santa Stocking Holder can be created following the same basic instructions as this Snowman Stocking Holder. Experiment with different patterns and decorating ideas.)

Snowman Stocking Holder

MATERIALS

Cotton fabric: $^1/_2$" bias strip, torn
Buttons: black (3), ivory (2)
Thin twine
Acrylic paints: black, dk. brown, dk. gold, dk. gray-blue, hunter green, ivory, dk. peach, bright red, and white
Acrylic matte spray sealer
Permanent marker, ultra-fine: black
Pine board: $^3/_4$" x 18" x 7" (1), 1" x 3" x 3" (1)
Plywood: $^1/_4$" (8" x 5")
Twigs: 7" (2 for arms), 3" (about 20, very thin)
Miniature birdhouse
Miniature pail
Miniature cookie cutter mittens: 2
Small wooden stars: 4
Artificial pine pick
Purchased stocking holder (model is a tin pine tree)

GENERAL SUPPLIES

Drill with $^1/_4$" drill bit
Glue: craft and wood

Paintbrushes
Sandpaper
Saw
Toothbrush

INSTRUCTIONS

1. Snowman body is cut from $^3/_4$" pine, stand is cut from 1" pine, and accents are cut from plywood. Enlarge patterns (opposite page) 200%. Transfer patterns onto appropriate wood and cut out. Drill arm holes in upper part of body large enough to insert twigs.

2. Paint snowman as in diagram (right), or as desired. Diluting the paint with a little water gives the project a softer look. When paint is dry, add detail with black marker.

3. Glue buttons to coat, pocket and hat. Tie two bows with twine and attach with craft glue to hat and pocket buttons. Use wood glue to attach hat, scarf, pocket, and twig arms to body.

4. Make a thin paint wash with dark brown paint and water. Brush onto entire surface of snowman. Dip a toothbrush into white paint.

DIAGRAM

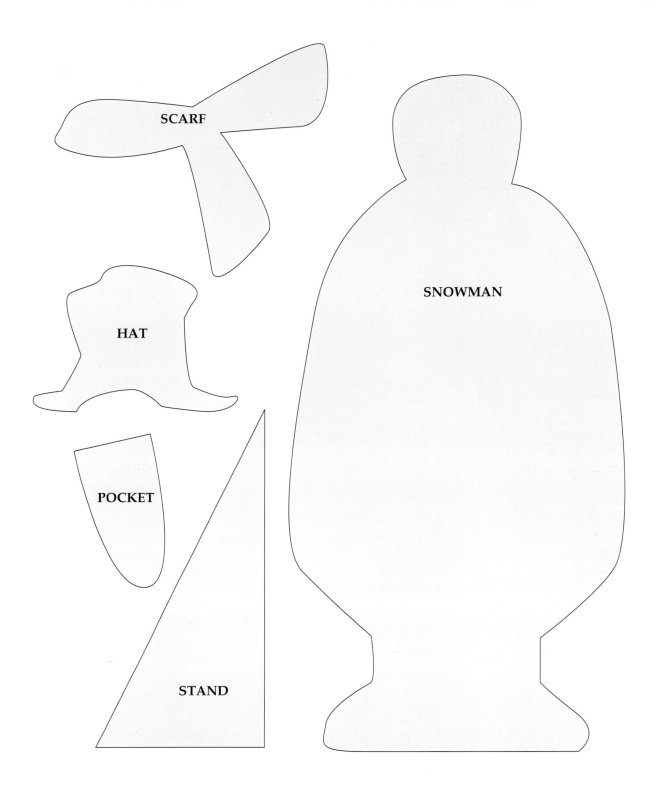

SCARF

HAT

POCKET

STAND

SNOWMAN

ENLARGE PATTERNS 200%

Jo Packham 113

Large Stockings

MATERIALS

(For one large stocking)
Stocking fabric: 1 1/2 yd.
Flannel fabric: 3/4 yd.
Fabric scraps for applique: checks,
    plaids, solids (refer to pattern
    on opposite page for print
    designs and colors)
Fusible webbing: 1/3 yd.
Matching thread
Embroidery floss: black and tan
Assorted buttons and beads
Twine: 2 yds.

GENERAL SUPPLIES

Iron and ironing board
Scissors
Sewing machine
Sewing needle
Tracing paper

INSTRUCTIONS

1.   Enlarge desired pattern (opposite page) 400%. Trace individual patterns onto tracing paper. From stocking fabric, cut out four stocking shapes. From flannel, cut out two stocking shapes. Set aside.

2.   From traced paper patterns, cut out individual pieces. Trace these patterns onto paper side of fusible webbing. Cut out fusible patterns following the general shape, not the exact line. Iron individual patterns onto appropriate fabric scraps. Cut out exact patterns from fabrics.

3.   For stocking front, place one stocking fabric pattern and one flannel pattern with right sides together. Sew a 1/4" seam around edges, leaving top open. Clip curves and turn right side out. Repeat for back.

4.   Place flannel lined front and back pieces with right sides together and sew a 1/4" seam around edges, leaving top open. Clip curves and turn right side out.

5.   Iron patterns onto front of stocking, referring to photo (left) for placement.

6.   Stitch buttons and twine on stocking. Finish face with black embroidery floss and beads. Hand-stitch outlines with tan floss.

7.   For hanger, cut an 8" x 2" rectangle from stocking fabric. Align long edges with right sides together and stitch. Turn right side out and press.

8.   For lining, sew remaining two stocking shapes with right sides together, leaving top and 3" at toe area open. Do not turn.

9.   Slip lining over top of stocking and align top raw edges. Bring raw edges of hanger together to form a loop. Insert hanger into stocking at left corner between lining and stocking. Loop should point downward. Sew around top edge of stocking.

10.   Pull stocking out through hole in lining. Stitch opening in lining closed and tuck into stocking. ❧

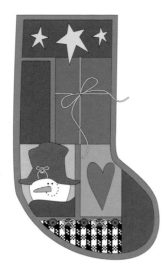

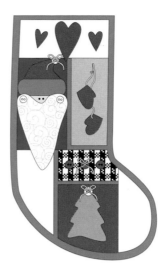

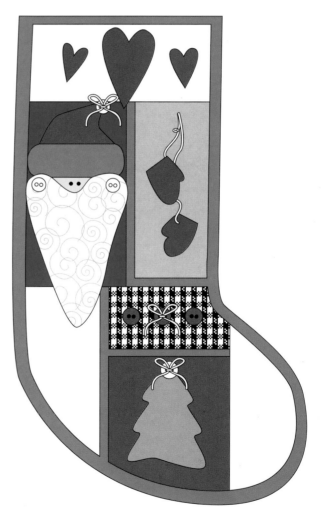

ENLARGE PATTERNS 400%

Log Cabin

Materials

Pine board #2: $^3/_4$" x 6' x 1'
Half rounds: $^5/_{16}$" x $^5/_8$" x 20' (1),
    $^1/_2$" x 1" x 35' (1)
Finishing nails
Wood stain: desired color (optional)

General supplies

Hammer
Sandpaper
Saw
Tracing paper
Wood glue

Instructions

1. Enlarge patterns (right) 400%. From pine, cut out two sides, one front, one back, two roof pieces, and a 7" x 11" piece for bottom. Sand all edges.

2. Assemble house by nailing and gluing front and back between sides. Drop bottom inside and nail and glue into place. Nail and glue a roof piece on each side. (Note: The top of roof piece is the open end.)

3. Once house is assembled, half rounds are attached with wood glue to resemble logs. From the

larger half rounds, cut twenty-four 8 $^1/_2$" pieces, thirteen 2 $^1/_2$" pieces, ten 1 $^3/_8$" pieces, five 11" pieces, four 9" pieces, four 6" pieces, two 13 $^1/_4$" pieces, two 4 $^1/_2$" pieces, and one 5" piece. From the smaller half rounds, cut twenty-four 8 $^1/_2$" pieces. The smaller logs will be used on the roof.

4. To cover back of house, work from bottom to top in the following order: 11" log, 11" log, three 2 $^1/_2$" logs on each side of windows, and top with an 11" log. (Note: Logs do not go completely to top of wood.) Glue a 6" log vertically to each side of back, flush with bottom.

5. To cover front of house, work from bottom to top in the following order: 11" log, a 4 $^1/_2$" log on each side of doorway, three 1 $^3/_8$" logs on outside of each window, two 1 $^3/_8$" logs on each side of doorway, one 5" log on top of doorway, and 11" log on top. (Note: Logs do not go completely to top of wood.) Glue a 6" log vertically to each side of front, flush with bottom.

6. To cover sides of house, place twelve 8 $^1/_2$" logs in a row, flat side up, onto work surface. Place a paper pattern of the house side over logs and trace peak. Cut logs accordingly. Repeat for other side of house. Glue logs into position.

7. Cover roof with smaller 8 $^1/_2$" logs, gluing four to each section. Cover sides of roof with 9" larger logs. Glue 13" larger logs to bottom overhang of roof. Glue two 2 $^1/_2$" larger logs together and glue into position on each roof peak. Stain house if desired. ❧

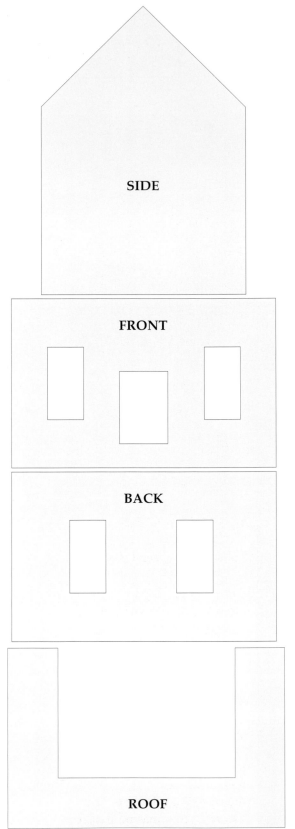

ENLARGE PATTERNS 400%

Revolving Reindeer Music Box

MATERIALS

Velvet fabric: green ($^1/_4$ yd.),
    red ($^1/_4$ yd.)
Muslin fabric: $^1/_8$ yd.
Velour fabric: brown ($^1/_4$ yd.),
    tan ($^1/_8$ yd.)
Ribbon: $^3/_4$" wide, black/metallic
    gold ($^1/_2$ yd.); $^1/_4$" wide,
    green (1 $^1/_2$ yds.)
Flat braid: $^1/_4$" wide, gold (1 $^1/_2$ yds.)
Fusible webbing: 8" x 11" (2 pcs.)
Fusible tear-away: 8" x 11" (2 pcs.)
Stuffing
Matching thread
Bugle beads: 2
Miniature jingle bells: 6
Assorted Christmas miniatures
Music box with turntable: 2" wide
Mat board: 12" square

GENERAL SUPPLIES

Beading needle
Drill with $^3/_8$" and $^1/_4$" drill bits
Hot glue gun and glue sticks
Iron and ironing board
Screwdriver
Scissors
Sewing machine

INSTRUCTIONS

All seams are $^1/_4$".

1.   Enlarge patterns (page 118) 200% and 400% as indicated, transferring all information. From red velvet, cut two music box covers. From tan velour, cut two pack pouches and two back packs; set aside. From mat board, cut two bases; set aside. From green velvet, cut one base, adding $^1/_4$" seam allowance; set aside. From muslin, cut two 5" x 4" pieces.

2.   Transfer reindeer to paper side of fusible webbing; draw one reindeer. Reverse pattern; draw second reindeer. Fuse rough side of webbing to wrong side of brown velour. Cut out one reindeer. Remove paper. Position reindeer on one music box cover, matching back and tail edges and with head and antlers extending above velvet; see diagram (page 118). Fuse. Repeat with second reindeer.

3.   Transfer antlers outline to paper side of fusible webbing; draw one set of antlers. Fuse rough side of webbing antlers to one 5" x 4" piece of muslin. Cut out antlers. Remove paper. Position muslin antlers on wrong side of matching brown velour antlers, aligning edges. Fuse. Reverse pattern; draw second set of antlers on fusible webbing and repeat on remaining muslin piece and brown velour antlers. Muslin will reinforce antlers when they are stuffed.

4.   Place shiny side of one sheet of tear-away against wrong side of red velvet; press. Machine satin-stitch around reindeer with matching thread according to pattern. To remove tear-away, lift at one corner and carefully tear. To remove from applique, make a small scissor cut in portion of tear-away backing reindeer; lift and tear.

5.   With right sides facing, sew music box cover pieces together, leaving opening between antlers and in back seam according to pattern. Also leave bottom open. Do not turn.

6.   Measure around bottom edge of music box cover. From green velvet, cut a 2 $^1/_2$"-wide strip

to fit around bottom edge, including seam allowance. With right sides facing, sew short ends together, then sew strip to bottom edge of cover. Cut small hole in center of velvet base according to pattern. Sew green velvet base to bottom of velvet strip. Turn cover through opening in back seam.

7.   Stuff antlers and head firmly. To make eyes, sew one bugle bead to each side of reindeer face, pulling thread tightly enough to indent fabric. Slip-stitch opening between antlers closed.

8.   Drill one $^3/_8$" hole through center of each mat board base according to pattern. Remove music box turntable. Insert music box winder stem through center of one base. Mark location of music box screws on base. Drill $^1/_4$" holes through screw locations. Repeat with remaining base. Hot-glue bases together, matching holes. Remove screws from music box.

Insert music box winder stem through center of mat board base. Insert screws and secure music box in place.

9.   With winder stem facing down, insert mat board base into cover through opening in back seam. Insert winder stem through hole in velvet base. Screw turntable to stem. Stuff reindeer music box firmly. Slip-stitch opening closed.

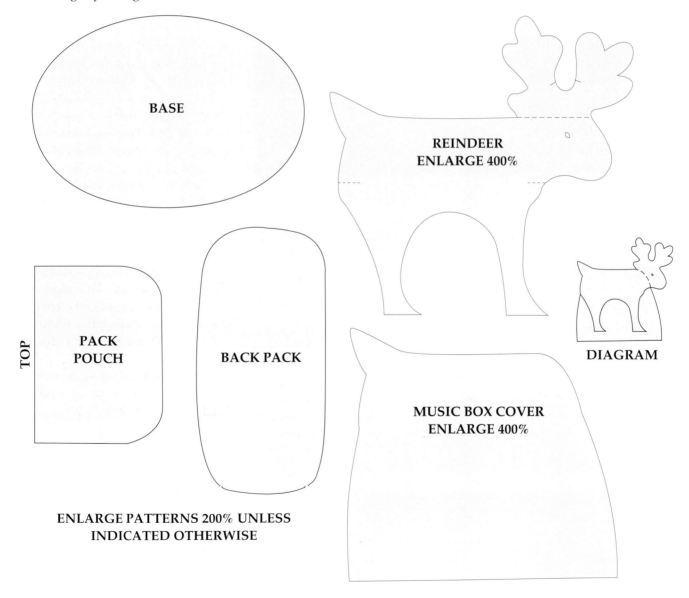

BASE

REINDEER
ENLARGE 400%

TOP

PACK
POUCH

BACK PACK

DIAGRAM

MUSIC BOX COVER
ENLARGE 400%

ENLARGE PATTERNS 200% UNLESS INDICATED OTHERWISE

10. Measure and cut one length of black/metallic gold ribbon and three lengths of flat gold braid to fit snugly around music box cover. Glue around cover; see photo (page 117).

11. To make packs, fold top 1" of pack pouch to wrong side; tack in place. Slightly gather lower edge of pouch to match back pack. With wrong side of pouch facing right side of one back pack, sew pouch to one end of back pack. Repeat with remaining pouch at opposite end of one back pack. With right sides facing, sew back packs together, leaving an opening. Turn. Slip-stitch opening closed. Tack packs to reindeer back.

12. From green ribbon, cut one 12" length. To make halter, fold ribbon in half, forming a 3" loop in the center and crisscrossing ribbon tails. Slide loop over reindeer nose and secure under chin with bead of glue where tails cross. Thread three bells onto each ribbon tail, spacing bells $3/4$" apart. Glue halter at back of neck; trim excess ribbon. Cut remaining ribbon into two equal lengths. Tie each length into a bow. Glue knots of bows to back of neck, over halter.

13. Fill packs with Christmas miniatures. ❧

Tree Skirt

Materials

Heavy-weave fabric: natural (1 yd.), red (1 yd.)
Muslin: 1 yd.
Buttons to cover: $7/8$" dia. (5)
Matching thread

General supplies

Iron and ironing board
Scissors
Sewing machine
Sewing needle
Straight pins

Instructions

1. Cut one 36" circle from natural fabric and muslin. Find center of fabric circles by folding in half and in half again. Crease center and unfold. Cut a 2" circle in center of both pieces. On one side, cut a slit from edge to center. Set aside.

2. Cut one 36" circle from red fabric. Measure and mark 4" in from outer edge and cut. The outer circle is the one that will be used.

3. Cut two 4" x $17^{1}/_{2}$" plackets from natural fabric and two 4" x $17^{1}/_{2}$" plackets from muslin.

4. Place one natural placket down right side of slit in natural circle with right sides together. Sew a $3/8$" seam. Fold placket out and press. Repeat with one muslin placket on muslin circle.

5. Mark $2^{1}/_{2}$" from outer edge of natural circle. Pin inside edge of red circle along mark on natural circle, with right sides together. Left side of red circle will not come completely around. Sew together with a $3/8$" seam. Fold red piece down and press, clipping curves if necessary.

6. Place muslin circle and natural circle with right sides together. Starting on left side of inner circle, sew a seam around circle, down right side of slit, and around outer edge. Leave left slit open. Turn right side out and press.

7. Place remaining muslin and natural plackets with wrong sides together. Serge together along right edge. Stitch top and bottom edges under. Pin left edge of placket to left edge of skirt with right sides together. Sew a seam. Fold placket out and press. Turn serged edge of placket under until edge crosses seam line. Stitch down seam line.

8. Stitch around top seam line between red trim and natural skirt. Stitch down seam line on right placket.

9. Cover four buttons with natural fabric and one button with red fabric. Sew buttons onto left placket with red button on bottom. Mark placement of buttonholes on right placket. Hand-sew button holes. ❧

Large Knit Christmas Tree Stocking

MATERIALS

Wool blend sports weight yarn:
   green (146 yds.)
Wool blend sports weight yarn:
   brown (5 yds.)
Worsted weight wool yarn:
   off- white (2 skeins)

GENERAL SUPPLIES

Double pointed knitting needles:
   12" long, size 7 (set of four)
Crochet hook: size G
Yarn needle: size 13

INSTRUCTIONS

Gauge: 5 sts = 1", 6 rows = 1"
**SKP = slip 1, k 1, pass the slipped
   st over.**
St st = stockinette st.

Use 2 needles until Row 77.
Cuff: cast on 101 sts.
Row 1: work rib k 1, (p 1, k 1)
across.
Row 2: p 1, (k 1, p 1) across.
Repeat these 2 rows alternating
until 36 rows (approx 6") have been
completed.
Row 37: k across.
Row 38: p across.
Row 39: k across.
Row 40: p across.
Continue working in St st. k across
50 sts. Place a marker on needle.
Begin working row 1 of chart
(opposite page) across next 51 sts.
Continue to follow chart, dec 1 st
each end of rows 69 and 71 = 97 sts.
Work 2 rows of St st, (p 1 row, k 1
row).
Dec row: dec 13 sts evenly spaced
across next row = 84 sts.
Ankle: continue working in St st for
3 rows more. Dec 1 st each end of
next row. Rep these last 4 rows
twice more = 78 sts.
Purl 1 row.
Joining rnd: Knit to last 19 sts, drop
yarn, with a piece of contrasting
yarn k these last 19 sts, place a
marker on needle for center heel
join, working in rnds from this
point, k next 19 sts on same needle
for heel, (this yarn will later be
removed to produce live sts to be
picked up to work heel). Sl
remaining 40 sts onto 2 needles for
instep, break off contrasting yarn,
pick up yarn and k across same 38
sts worked with contrasting yarn.
Work in St st (k every rnd) for 6 rnds.
Decrease rnd: work to last 2 sts
before center heel marker, k 2 tog, sl

marker, k 2 tog, complete the
around.
Next rnd: k around.
Rep these last 2 rnds twice more =
72 sts.
K 14 rnds.
Toe: Divide sts for toe as follows: sl
last 2 sts just worked to free needle,
with same needle k across 16 sts to
marker. With another needle, work
next 16 sts, work 2 more sts from
next needle. With another needle,
work across 36 instep sts, k to
marker.
Dec rnd: k to within 3 sts of end of
first needle, which is the next
needle, k 2 tog, k 1, second needle,
k 1, sl 1, k 1, psso, k to within 3 sts
of end, k 2 tog, k 1, third needle, k
1, sl 1, k 1, psso, k 15.
K one rnd.
Rep these 2 rnds alternating 4 times
more = 52 sts.
Work dec rnd only, until 16 sts
remain.
K 4 sts of first needle, sl them to
third needle. Leave a tail of yarn 18"
long, break off. Weave sole and
instep sts tog.
Heel: from this point, stocking will
be joined and worked in rnds. Pull
out contrasting yarn. Pick up 19 sts
on each side of marker on two
needles for sole, pick up 38 sts
along instep, pick up one loop each
end of instep. Right side facing,
fasten yarn to first st on right hand
side of marker, k 18 sts, sl first st of
second needle to first needle, k 2
tog, k to within one st of end of next
needle, sl first st of third needle to
second needle, k 2 tog, k to end of
rnd. There will be 19 sts on first and
third needles and 38 on second
needle. K 2 rnds.
Dec rnd: k to within 2 sts of end of
first needle, k 2 tog, second needle,
k 2 tog, k to within 2 sts of end of
needle, k 2 tog; third needle, k 2
tog, k to end. K 1 rnd. Rep last 2

rnds until 14 sts remain. K 7 sts of first needle, slip them to third needle. Leave a tail of yarn 24" long, break off. Weave sts tog.

Tie for hanging stocking:
With size G crochet hook, chain 50. Turn ch wrong side up. Work sc in single loops of each ch. Fasten off. Sew to center back of stocking. ❧

Clothespin Snowmen

MATERIALS

(For one snowman)
Wool fabric: $3/8$" x 7"
Acrylic paints: black, orange, off-white
Acrylic gloss spray sealer
Round peg clothespin: $3 3/4$" long
Wooden wheel: $3/4$" dia.
Thread spool: $1/2$"

GENERAL SUPPLIES

Paintbrush
Wood glue

INSTRUCTIONS

1.   Glue thread spool to center of wheel and let dry.

2.   Paint clothespin with two coats of off-white paint and let dry.

3.   Paint spool black, forming hat. Dot eyes, mouth, and buttons onto clothespin snowman with black paint. Paint an orange carrot nose. Let dry.

4.   Glue hat to top of snowman. Let dry.

5.   Spray with gloss sealer.

6.   Fray edges of wool fabric and tie in a double knot around snowman's neck. ❧

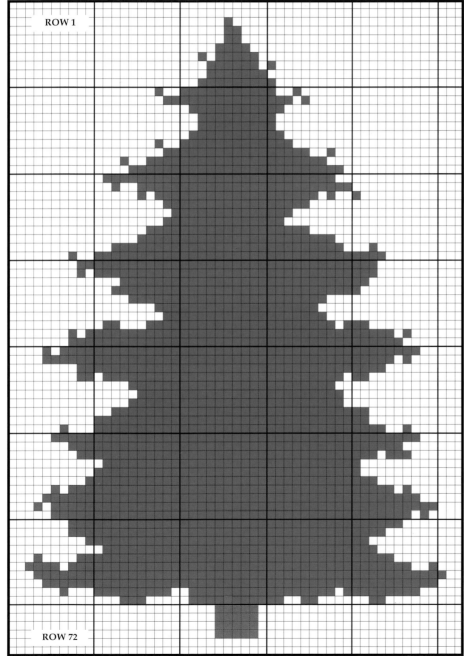

ROW 1

ROW 72

ONE SQUARE EQUALS ONE STITCH

Small Stocking

MATERIALS

(For brown stocking)
Also shown: gray and wine
Wool sports weight yarn: brown
(146 yds.)

GENERAL SUPPLIES

Double pointed knitting needles: 6"
long, size 2 (set of 5)
Crochet hook: size F

INSTRUCTIONS

Gauge: 6 sts = 1", 9 rows = 1"
SKP= slip 1, k 1, pass the slipped
st over and off needle.
St st = stockinette st.

Cast on 42 sts.
Use 2 needles. Work in St st (p 1
row, k 1 row) for 9 rows.
Next row: Right side. k 1, (yo, k 2
tog) across to last st, yo k 1 = 43 sts.
Next row: p 2 tog, p across = 42 sts.
Work St st (k 1 row, p 1 row) for 66
rows.
Next row: k to last 10 sts.
Heel (work in rnds): With a short
piece of yarn of a different color
and another needle, k last 10 sts and
10 sts at beg of row for heel joining
stocking, drop contrasting yarn.

Slip next 11 sts to another needle,
slip the next 11 sts to another
needle for a total of 22 sts for instep.
With fourth needle, pick up yarn
and k the same 20 sts of heel
worked with contrasting color, k 22
instep sts. Continue working for 20
rnds in St st (k every round) for 2 1/4".
Toe (beg rnds at center back heel):
place next 10 sts on first needle, 22
sts of instep on second needle, 10
sts on third needle. k 10, SKP, k 18,
k 2 tog, k 10.
Next rnd (dec rnd): k to within 3 sts
of end of first needle, k 2 tog, k 1;
on second needle, k 1 sl 1, k 1, psso,
k to within 3 sts of end, k 2 tog, k 1;
on third needle, k 1, sl 1, k 1, psso, k
to end.
K 1 rnd.
Rep last 2 rnds twice more.
Rep dec rnd every rnd until 12 sts
remain, k 3 sts from first needle and
sl them to third needle. Weave sole
and instep sts tog.
Heel: Pull out colored yarn for heel
sts, beg at center back, pick up 10
live sts on first needle, pick up an
extra loop at instep, pick up 20 live
sts on second needle, on third
needle pick up an extra loop at
instep, pick up 10 live sts to center
back = 42. Join yarn at center back,
first needle, k 9, k 2 tog; second
needle, k 20; third needle k 2 tog, k
9.
K 1 rnd.
Dec rnd: k to within 2 sts of end of
first needle, k 2 tog; second needle,
k 2 tog, k to last 2 sts, k 2 tog; third
needle, k 2 tog; k to end.
Next row: k 1 rnd.
Rep these last 2 rnds, alternating
until 16 sts remain. k 4 sts from first
needle and slip them to third
needle. Weave sts tog as for toe.
Sew back of stocking tog.
Turn hem at top of stocking to
wrong side 8 rows down and
whipstitch in place.

Make a chain loop (double yarn)
approximately 20 sts or 3" long and
join to center back of stocking for
hanging. ✥

Knit Mitten

MATERIALS

Wool blend sports weight yarn: dk.
green (292 yds.)

GENERAL SUPPLIES

Double pointed knitting needles: 7"
long, size 3 (set of 4)

INSTRUCTIONS

(For two mittens)
Gauge: approximately 5 sts = 1", 7
rows = 1"
SKP = slip 1 st, k 1 st, pass slipped
st over and off needle.

Cuff: Cast on 46 sts. Divide sts onto
3 needles as follows: 16 sts on first
needle, 14 sts on second needle, 16
sts on third needle.
Rnds 1–11: k around.
Rnd 12: (yo, k 2 tog.) around.
Rnds 13-24: k around

Hand: Work in garter st.
Rnd 25: p around.
Rnd 26: k around.
Rnds 27–37: rep rnds 25 and 26
alternating, 6 times more, end with
rnd 25, a p rnd.

Opening for thumb: Rnd 38: k 1,
increase in next st, k to last 2 sts of
rnd, inc in next st, k 1 = 48 sts.
Rnd 39: p.
Rnd 40: k 2, inc in next st, k to last 3
sts of rnd, inc in next st, k 2 = 50 sts.

Rnd 41: p.
Rnd 42: k 3, inc in next st, k to last 4 sts of rnd, inc in next st, k 3 = 52 sts.
Rnd 43: p.
Rnd 44: k 4, inc in next st, k to last 5 sts of rnd, inc in next st, k 4 = 54 sts.
Rnd 45: p.
Rnd 46: k 5, inc in next st, k to last 6 sts of rnd, inc in next st, k 5 = 56 sts.
Rnd 47: p.
Rnd 48: k 6, inc in next st, k to last 7 sts of rnd, inc in next st, k 6 = 58 sts.
Rnd 49: p.
Rnd 50: k 7, inc in next st, k to last 8 sts of rnd, inc in next st, k 7 = 60 sts.
Rnd 51: p.
Rnd 52: k 8, inc in next st, k to last 9 sts of rnd, inc in next st, k 8 = 62 sts.
Rnd 53: p.
Rnd 54: k 9, inc in next st, k to last 10 sts of rnd, inc in next st, k 9 = 64 sts.
Rnd 55: p.
Rnd 56: k 10, inc in next st, k to last 11 sts of rnd, inc in next st, k 10 = 66 sts.
Break off yarn. Slip last 10 st worked to a holder. Slip next 10 sts to a holder. These 20 sts will be worked later to complete thumb.

Hand: Rnds 1–35: join yarn in next st, p 46 sts around. Continue in rounds on these 46 sts in garter st, k 1 rnd, p 1 rnd, until 35 rnds are completed from beginning of hand, end with a p rnd.
Rnd 36: k 10, k 2 tog, k 22, SKP, k 10 = 44 sts.
Rnd 37 and every odd numbered rdn: p.
Rnd 38: k 8, k 2 tog, k 2, SKP, k 16, k 2 tog, k 2, SKP, k 8 = 40 sts.
Rnd 40: k 7, k 2 tog, k 2, SKP, k 14, k 2 tog, k 2, SKP, k 7 = 36 sts.
Rnd 42: k 6, k 2 tog, k 2, SKP, k 12, k 2 tog, k 2, SKP, k 6 = 32 sts.
Rnd 44: k 5, k 2 tog, k 2, SKP, k 10, k 2 tog, k 2, SKP, k 5 = 28 sts.
Rnd 46: k 4, k 2 tog, k 2, SKP, k 8, k 2 tog, k2, SKP, k 4 = 24 sts.
Rnd 48: k 3, k 2 tog, k 2, SKP, k 6, k 2 tog, k 2, SKP, k 3 = 20 sts.
Rnd 50: k 2, k 2 tog, k 2, SKP, k 4, k 2 tog, k 2, SKP, k 2 = 16 sts.
Break off yarn. Place first and last 4 sts onto one needle, place other 8 sts on another needle. Weave these sts together from wrong side of work to keep pattern.

Thumb: Place 20 sts from holder onto 3 needles.
Rnd 1: p.
Rnd 2: k.
Rep rnds 1 and 2 alternating, until 20 rnds are complete. Leave a 10" tail of yarn, break off. Thread tail through needle and run through all 20 sts. Pull tightly, gathering all sts. Fasten off.

Cuff hem: Fold on rnd 12 and whipstitch to rnd 24. ❧

Snowman Ornament

MATERIALS

Wool fabric scrap: $^3/_4$" x 11"
Thin cording: gold (7")
Small velvet poinsettia
Acrylic paints: black, orange, and off-white
Acrylic gloss spray sealer
Wooden knob: 2 $^1/_4$" (1), 2" (1)
Wooden bead: 35mm
Wooden thread spool: 1"
Wooden wheel: 1 $^1/_2$"

GENERAL SUPPLIES

Glue: industrial-strength and wood
Paintbrush

INSTRUCTIONS

1.   Glue flat sides of knobs together with wood glue. Glue bead on top of 2" knob, forming snowman. Glue spool to center of wheel. Let dry.

2.   Paint snowman with two coats of off-white and let dry. Paint spool black, forming hat. Paint black dots for eyes, mouth, and buttons. Paint an orange carrot nose. Let dry.

3.   Fold gold cording in half and tie ends together with a knot. Slide cording through the bottom of wheel and up through spool so that the knot is at the bottom of the hat. Glue hat to the top of snowman's head and let dry.

4.   Spray snowman with gloss sealer. Let dry. Fray edges of wool and tie in a double knot around snowman's neck. With industrial-strength glue, attach poinsettia. ❧

Turtleneck Sweater

MATERIALS

Wool blend yarn: blue-gray tweed
(1 skein)

GENERAL SUPPLIES

Double pointed knitting needles: 7"
long, size 3 (set of 4)
Yarn needle: size 13

INSTRUCTIONS

**Gauge: approximately 5 sts = 1",
7 rows = 1"**
St st = stockinette st.
**The sweater is worked as one
piece. Work from the bottom-edge
front, to the bottom-edge back.**

Body: Cast on 19 sts. Work rib as
follows:
Row 1: k 1, (p 1, k 1) across.
Row 2: p 1, (k 1, p 1) across.
Rows 3-5: rept rows 1 and 2
alternating, end with row 1.
Row 6: k.
Row 7: p.
Rows 8-19: rept rows 6 and 7
alternating for 12 rows.

Sleeves: Row 20: cast on 10 sts, K
across=29 sts.
Row 21: cast on 10 sts, p across=39
sts.
Rows 22-27: work in St st for 6 rows.
Neck shaping-left side: Row 28: k
17, slip next 5 sts to a holder, join
another piece of yarn for right side,
k 17. Work both sides at same time.
Row 29: p 15, p 2 tog, drop yarn on
right side, pick up yarn on left side,
p 2 tog, p 15.
Row 30: k 14, k 2 tog, drop yarn,
pick up other yarn, k 2 tog, k 14.
Row 31: p 15, drop yarn, pick up
other yarn, p 15.
Row 32: k 15, drop yarn, pick up
other yarn, k 15.
Row 33: p 15, break yarn, pick up
yarn, p 15. Work with one yarn.
Row 34: k 15, cast on 9 for neck, k
15.
Row 35: p (39 sts).
Rows 36-43: work in St st for 8 rows.
Row 44: bind off 10 sts, k 29 sts.
Row 45: bind off 10 sts, p 19 sts.
Rows 46-59: work in St st for 14
rows.
Rows 60-64: work rib of k 1, p 1.
Bind off in rib.
Neck: right side facing, work in
rounds, join yarn to left shoulder,
pick up and k 7 sts to front, k 5 sts
from holder, pick up and knit 7 sts
to right shoulder, pick up and k 9
sts across back=28 sts. Divide onto 3
needles.
Rnds 1-10: k 1, p 1, rib around. Bind
off loosely in rib.
Cuffs: right side facing, join yarn to
first st, work along side edge of
sleeve, pick up and k a stitch in
every other sts across=14sts.
Rows 1-5: (k 1, p 1) rib across. Bind
off.

Sew sleeve and side seams together.
Roll neck ribbing to right side for
turtleneck. ❧

Topiary Trees for Painted Pots

MATERIALS

Painted pot (see opposite page)
Green foliage picks: 40–50 (the
    fuller the picks, the less needed)
Styrofoam cone: 13" high
Wooden dowel: $1/4$" x 9"
Plaster of Paris

GENERAL SUPPLIES

Craft glue
Masking tape
Pencil
Wire cutters

INSTRUCTIONS

1.   Tape off hole in bottom of pot
to seal. Prepare plaster following
manufacturer's instructions. Fill pot
with plaster up to 1" from the top.
Insert dowel into center of plaster. If
needed, place tape from edge of pot
to dowel to hold in place until set.

2.   Mark center bottom of cone by
inserting pencil 2" into foam,
remove pencil. Cover end of dowel
with craft glue. Position cone onto
dowel and slide down until bottom
rests on plaster. Let
glue dry completely.

3   Starting at the
bottom of the cone,
insert picks at the same
angle; see diagram
(right). Trim ends as
needed with wire
cutters. Consistent pick
lengths make a more
proportioned tree. ❧   **DIAGRAM**

Painted Pots

Materials

(For one pot)
Clay pot: (model is 6 $^1/_2$" high)
Acrylic paints: desired colors
Acrylic matte or gloss spray sealer

General Supplies

Graphite paper
Paintbrushes

Instructions

1.   Paint pot with a base coat if desired. Enlarge desired pattern to desired size and transfer onto pot with graphite paper.

2.   When painting background designs onto pots, thin paint with water. Paint designs following patterns or as desired.

3.   Painted pots can be antiqued by brushing a brown wash over entire pot, or add sparkle by spraying lightly with glitter.

4.   When paint is dry, spray pot with acrylic sealer in either matte or gloss finish, as desired. ❧

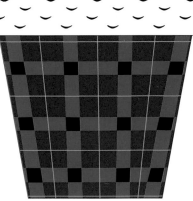

**ENLARGE PATTERNS TO
DESIRED SIZE**

PATTERNS

METRIC EQUIVALENCE CHART

MM-Millimetres   CM-Centimetres
INCHES TO MILLIMETRES AND CENTIMETRES

INCHES	MM	CM	INCHES	CM	INCHES	CM
⅛	3	0.3	9	22.9	30	76.2
¼	6	0.6	10	25.4	31	78.7
½	13	1.3	12	30.5	33	83.8
⅝	16	1.6	13	33.0	34	86.4
¾	19	1.9	14	35.6	35	88.9
⅞	22	2.2	15	38.1	36	91.4
1	25	2.5	16	40.6	37	94.0
1¼	32	3.2	17	43.2	38	96.5
1½	38	3.8	18	45.7	39	99.1
1¾	44	4.4	19	48.3	40	101.6
2	51	5.1	20	50.8	41	104.1
2½	64	6.4	21	53.3	42	106.7
3	76	7.6	22	55.9	43	109.2
3½	89	8.9	23	58.4	44	111.8
4	102	10.2	24	61.0	45	114.3
4½	114	11.4	25	63.5	46	116.8
5	127	12.7	26	66.0	47	119.4
6	152	15.2	27	68.6	48	121.9
7	178	17.8	28	71.1	49	124.5
8	203	20.3	29	73.7	50	127.0

YARDS TO METRES

YARDS	METRES	YARDS	METRES	YARDS	METRES	YARDS	METRES	YARDS	METRES
⅛	0.11	2⅛	1.94	4⅛	3.77	6⅛	5.60	8⅛	7.43
¼	0.23	2¼	2.06	4¼	3.89	6¼	5.72	8¼	7.54
⅜	0.34	2⅜	2.17	4⅜	4.00	6⅜	5.83	8⅜	7.66
½	0.46	2½	2.29	4½	4.11	6½	5.94	8½	7.77
⅝	0.57	2⅝	2.40	4⅝	4.23	6⅝	6.06	8⅝	7.89
¾	0.69	2¾	2.51	4¾	4.34	6¾	6.17	8¾	8.00
⅞	0.80	2⅞	2.63	4⅞	4.46	6⅞	6.29	8⅞	8.12
1	0.91	3	2.74	5	4.57	7	6.40	9	8.23
1⅛	1.03	3⅛	2.86	5⅛	4.69	7⅛	6.52	9⅛	8.34
1¼	1.14	3¼	2.97	5¼	4.80	7¼	6.63	9¼	8.46
1⅜	1.26	3⅜	3.09	5⅜	4.91	7⅜	6.74	9⅜	8.57
1½	1.37	3½	3.20	5½	5.03	7½	6.86	9½	8.69
1⅝	1.49	3⅝	3.31	5⅝	5.14	7⅝	6.97	9⅝	8.80
1¾	1.60	3¾	3.43	5¾	5.26	7¾	7.09	9¾	8.92
1⅞	1.71	3⅞	3.54	5⅞	5.37	7⅞	7.20	9⅞	9.03
2	1.83	4	3.66	6	5.49	8	7.32	10	9.14

INDEX